K S LAUKENBY

The Library of Pastoral Care

TITLES ALREADY PUBLISHED

Principles of Pastoral Counselling
R. S. Lee

Casework and Pastoral Care
Jean Heywood

In His Own Parish:
Pastoral Care through Parochial Visiting
Kenneth Child

Working with Children
Anthony Denney

Understanding the Adolescent
Michael Hare Duke

Marriage Preparation
Martin Parsons

Marriage Counselling
Kenneth Preston

Sick Call: A Book on the
Pastoral Care of the Physically Ill
Kenneth Child

Pastoral Care in Hospitals
Norman Autton

The Pastoral Care of the Mentally Ill
Norman Autton

Pastoral Care and the Drug Scene
Kenneth Leech

Caring for the Elderly
H. P. Steer

The Pastoral Care of the Dying
Norman Autton

The Pastoral Care of the Bereaved
Norman Autton

The Pastor and His Ministry
Owen Brandon

Library of Pastoral Care

THE PASTOR AND HIS MINISTRY

The Pastor
and His Ministry

OWEN BRANDON

LONDON

S·P·C·K

1972

First pubished in 1972
by S.P.C.K.
Holy Trinity Church,
Marylebone Road,
London, NWI 4DU

Made and printed in Great Britain by
William Clowes & Sons, Limited
London, Beccles, and Colchester

SBN 281 02661 0

Contents

ACKNOWLEDGEMENTS   viii

PREFACE   ix

1   The Ministry in Perspective:
    THE MINISTER AS SERVANT   1

2   Psychology and Religion:
    THE MINISTER AS INTERPRETER   8

3   Psychology Today:
    THE MINISTER AS LEARNER   16

4   Religious Development:
    THE MINISTER AS TEACHER   28

5   Psychology of Faith:
    THE MINISTER AS GUIDE   46

6   Psychology and Theology:
    THE MINISTER AS THEOLOGIAN   58

7   Prayer and Worship:
    THE MINISTER AS PRIEST   71

8   Caring and Sharing:
    THE MINISTER AS PASTOR   88

9   Postscript
    THE MINISTER AS PROFESSIONAL   99

NOTES   107

SUGGESTIONS FOR FURTHER STUDY   109

INDEX   115

Acknowledgements

Thanks are due for permission to quote from the following copyright sources:

The British Council of Churches: *Pastoral Care and the Training of Ministers: Contributions to a Developing Debate*, 1969.

Abingdon Press: *Profession: Minister*, by James D. Glasse, 1968.

Morehouse-Gorham Co: *What is the Priesthood? A Book on Vocation*, by John V. Butler and W. Norman Pittenger, 1954.

Preface

Within the present century the concept of the Christian Ministry, like many other concepts both secular and religious, has undergone a great change. During the past few decades there has been a growing uncertainty about the work of the ministry, and this has led to confusion and frustration, and in the case of some ministers, even to despair.

In January 1969, the Report of the Working Party entitled *Pastoral Care and the Training of Ministers: Contributions to a Developing Debate*, was published by the British Council of Churches. It makes the following comments:

> In modern Britain with its complex of welfare agencies the ordinand or the young minister often feels himself an amateur in a society of experts and professionals. He sees the doctor, teacher, probation officer, psychiatric social worker, child-care officer specially trained with the aid of modern knowledge and techniques to fulfil specific services to clients. He feels himself by contrast something of an odd man out serving an institution which in many urban and country districts hardly anybody seems to want. It does not seem that what he is required to do has for the most part any real relevance to the felt needs and experienced difficulties of men and women. In terms of social service, he is puzzled as to his exact function....
>
> The Christian community must take a long, cool, deep look at itself, at its understanding of its faith and function and at its expectations for the men whom it encourages, and assists to train for the specific tasks to which it calls them.
>
> The problem is so complex that it is difficult to know where to begin. Many issues cluster around it: the way we Christians interpret to ourselves what it is that we know

but others do not know; the way we evaluate and use what we have inherited, especially the Bible, doctrine, and liturgy; the kind of activities which local congregations regard as appropriate; the "deployment and payment" of ministers, their continuing education and their day-to-day programme—all this and much else contributes to this feeling of unease, of irrelevance, of ineffectiveness which the alert and sensitive young minister suffers.[1]

A former Bishop of Guildford preaching at a service of institution and induction began his sermon with the rhetorical questions, "What kind of man is your new vicar? What kind of man do you hope he is? You will want him to be not too 'high' and not too 'low'. You will want him to be a good visitor, a good preacher, a good organizer, a business man able to cope with the finances of the church, good with children and young people, good with old people and sick folk." Then he paused, leaned over the pulpit and said: "If you think like that you are hoping for a man God has never yet created!" Then he defined the work of the parish minister—to maintain the services of the church—to be a guide and example to his people—to be a man of God, giving of his best in every department of his ministry—supported by the prayers and loyalty of his people.

Now, whilst it is acknowledged that no man can be expert in everything, it is none the less evident, in spite of all the changes taking place in the Church, that the minister is expected to be efficient in a number of directions. A minister may approach his work from any of these directions, but it is helpful to him if he can see his work as one, and the various activities as aspects of that one ministry, and if he can adopt the approach most suited to his own personality and gifts as they relate to his own knowledge, training, and experience.

The present study offers notes on the psychological approach to the work of the ministry. It is both a study *about* and a study *within* the work of pastoral care. Perhaps before long new images or new models will be needed to describe the work of the ministry. No attempt is here made to create new models. The old models still have some relevance, so I have been content to speak of the minister as servant, teacher, guide, pastor, and have added a chapter on the developing concept of the minister as professional. The purpose of this study is not to create new models but to go behind familiar models in order to illustrate the relevance of the work of the ministry in this age. By using the basic term *minister* and adding to it some of the descriptive titles of familiar models, I have endeavoured to suggest both the essential unity and the functional diversity of his calling.

Two people who read this book in typescript remarked on the fact that it treats of many subjects in a small compass. One said, "Almost on every page I wanted to ask you to elaborate some point in the exposition." To treat of so many subjects in a small volume exposes an author to the danger of superficiality; but I have deliberately taken that risk for the sake of the reader. I would like to think of this as a book of ideas, a book to stimulate thought and discussion and to lead anyone who reads it to find fulfilment in the ministry in his own way. In that sense it is a stimulant rather than an exposition.

I thank the Reverend Dr Peter N. Brooks for reading the first draft typescript, for valuable comments on it, and for encouragement and help towards its publication. My thanks are due also to the Reverend Richard E. Parsons who kindly undertook to compile the Index.

For several years I have been in correspondence with the Reverend Dr James D. Glasse, President of Lancaster Theological Seminary, Pennsylvania, U.S.A., who has made a special study of the work of the ministry from the professional point of view, and I am grateful to him for permission to quote from his book, *Profession: Minister*, in my last chapter. About the time of the publication of the present work, it is hoped that Dr Glasse will have another book published taking his contribution to the subject a stage further. I regret that at the time of writing it is not possible to announce the title and date of Dr Glasse's new work or to use it in the present discussion.

1

The Ministry in Perspective
The Minister as Servant

The Church's task in any age is to relate to fluctuating social conditions and to changing concepts of human need. This is an age of inquiry, and in consequence is an undogmatic age. Dogma is out. Authoritative statements of all kinds are questioned, and it is fashionable to challenge and reject whatever ideas and theories are by nature unverifiable however well established they may be. Tradition is suspect, experiment is the order of the day.

This is the age of man. Evolution has carried man so far that now he is able to direct its course and determine where it shall lead. Interest in the scientific study of man and his life on this planet abounds; yet the more we know of human nature as exhibited in everyday life and behaviour, the more apparent it becomes that modern man is his own most acute problem. In one sense man is the central problem of the age. Science has given him many opportunities for a fuller life but his perplexity is how to use them.

The age of man is an age of expansion. People of my generation were born into a country. England was my homeland, other places were "overseas". Children of the generation which followed were born into the world. Travel facilities, television, the movement of people by emigration and immigration and the constant meeting of people of various races resulting from all these movements have made the world seem a smaller place than it was in my childhood days. Future generations will be born into the universe, with space travel a matter no longer to be wondered at. In future generations man will be the citizen of the universe.

The twentieth century is in some ways a wistful age. It is

an age in which many persons consciously feel that they have lost their way. Life seems so meaningless to many. There is so much to disappoint even at the moments of man's greatest achievements; and, without being too sombre, one cannot help being aware of widespread feelings of loss of bearing, lack of confidence, sadness, loneliness, heart-break, and despair; and at the same time a longing, a yearning for something better.

In spite of changing circumstances there are certain aspects of the Church's relation to the world which remain constant. One such aspect is the minister's role as servant. The work of the minister is sacred: he shares the joys and sorrows of others and helps to bear their burdens; he helps them to resolve their problems or to learn to accept what they cannot change and to adjust to it; he is entrusted with their confidence; he hears their confessions; at times he is the sole support of the dying and the bereaved. In short, the work of the minister is service. The very word means "servant"; and there are certain attitudes which a minister must adopt in order for his service to be effective. Six such attitudes are perhaps worthy of special consideration.

1. *Confidence.*   The minister needs confidence—confidence in himself—confidence in his calling—confidence in people —confidence in life—perhaps it is too obvious to add confidence in God. Many ministers are losing confidence—which is only another way of saying that they are losing faith. But this need not be. The ministry is a high calling. It is a privilege to be entrusted with the work it entails.

The minister's work is a unique work. He has a role and function in society that are uniquely his. This does not mean that there is no need for change in the exercise of his calling and no room for improvement in his professional training and status. Reforms and changes are urgently needed, but these are not relevant here. An immediate need is the restoration of confidence in the vocation and work of the ministry.

2. *Humility.*   Confidence needs to be balanced by humility, for the man with a strong sense of vocation is always in

danger of limiting his usefulness by over-confidence in his own ability and in the value of his own particular theological outlook. There is a temptation for the minister to feel that by virtue of his calling and training he has all the answers to everyone else's questions and problems.

I recall a conversation I had with a medical doctor, a general practitioner, on the subject of doctor–clergy co-operation. He said that at times he has met a patient who, he felt, needed the kind of help that a clergyman ought to be able to give. But he added: "What can I do? If I send a patient to the vicar at one end of my district I know what he will tell the patient. He will say, 'Come to Jesus'. And if I send that patient to the vicar at the other end of my district, he will say, 'Come to confession and the Eucharist'. They seem to have only one answer to every problem." This doctor—a devout Christian man himself—was not being facetious or unkind. He was commenting on a situation as he found it.

It is good for a minister sometimes to examine himself in respect of his dominant attitudes. Are all our convictions true convictions, or are some of them rationalized prejudices? Each one of us adopts a unique, personal, and individual point of view. That is natural. It is a psychological necessity. We cannot help it. But we need to remember that at best our point of view is partial: it cannot be all-embracing. Any individual's point of view on any matter is limited in at least three directions.

A point of view is limited to a knowledge of something less than the whole truth. From a single vantage-point no one can hope to see everything that there is to see. The theological controversies of history so often have been the altercations of men who have been looking at the same things from opposite points of view and who have failed to realize that there are aspects of truth which from their own limited standpoint they cannot see. Once an individual imagines that he can see the whole truth his thinking apparatus tends to become clogged; he is on his way to becoming intolerant. A little self-knowledge seasoned with humility might save him and others from painful wranglings.

Again, a point of view is limited in that it embraces only those elements of experience that can be discerned in consciousness; it takes little account of subconscious or unconscious motives, tensions, conflicts, or repressions.

This is a most important aspect of the problem. Recent studies in prejudice have demonstrated the deep-seated nature of the issue. Prejudice often has its roots in the unconscious depths of the mind. A man's conscious likes and dislikes are not always as rational as he supposes. More often than many people realize they are associated in the unconscious with irrational personal loves and hates. And this is as true of the minister as it is of anyone else.

Sometimes prejudice against another's point of view stems from fear. On the surface an intolerant person may appear to be quite certain of his ground. He speaks with assurance. He knows he is right. But does he know? His avowed position may well be a rationalization, an unconscious attempt to bolster up his opinions because in the ultimate issue (albeit not in full consciousness) he has doubts about their validity. The authoritarian type of personality may defend a position passionately, but the very passion may be indicative of an underlying uncertainty and fear. Sometimes a prejudiced person is unconsciously very near to accepting the point of view which he so vehemently attacks. His outward vehemence may be evidence of an inward unconscious turmoil.

Once more, a point of view is limited to making an appeal to something less than the whole community. This is obvious when stated thus, but it tends to be forgotten in some discussions about man and his needs and when the content and application of the gospel are under consideration.

Some ministers are at fault here. A pattern of belief or a form of behaviour associated with a particular religious in-group may be valid and satisfying for an individual or for a number of individuals within that in-group, but no one can expect his own particular patterns and forms to fit the needs of every other individual with whom he comes in contact. Objective thinking here would help a great deal in our relations with one another.

3. *Humanity.* Those engaged in the work of the ministry ought of all persons to be the most human. When I was about to undertake some specialized work amongst prisoners a few years ago I received two letters by the same post. In one the writer said: "I personally should find prison work fearfully depressing. I think the only chance of survival would be to treat the prisoners as 'cases' rather than as people. But it needs someone to do it." My other correspondent wrote: "Nothing could give greater satisfaction and fulfilment than to have a share in mending broken lives. One cannot help feeling that so many of these men are just like us, really, only more so. They perhaps have never had a sympathetic listener."

Whilst appreciating the feeling that lies behind the first letter, the attitude expressed in the second letter is the only possible attitude for one who undertakes a helping role of any kind. I remember a clergyman who was known to his friends as "a bit of a scholar" in what has been popularly called "an advanced theology". He was a man devoted to his work and to his people, and when he died the bishop of his diocese said about him: "His people may not always have understood his divinity but they could not fail to be touched by his humanity." Here is the authentic mark of the pastor.

4. *Understanding.* This flows from the spirit of humanity. Some people find it hard to understand others. The minister must cultivate a profound respect for other human persons. And I mean every word of that. Each individual is a self over against all other selves. We are all aware of ourselves as individuals, aware of our own existence, of our own needs, and perhaps of our own importance. So far so good, but we need to cultivate the habit of respecting other selves. I prefer to speak of others as persons rather than as people, for the word *person* seems to indicate something that is essential to them.

When I speak of respecting other persons I am not thinking of the "live and let live" attitude, but of something deeper and more fundamental.

We might consider Christ's attitude to individuals. The Gospels set him forth in his humanity as having a deep understanding of human nature. It was said of him that "he knew men so well, all of them, that he needed no evidence from others about a man, for he himself could tell what was in a man". He was at ease with all sorts and conditions of men. Children loved him. Needy folk turned to him. Wayward folk trusted him. People with problems confided in him. Why? Because of his profound respect for their humanity. In the main, those who felt uneasy in his presence were the self-righteous who knew that he could see through the sham of their hypocrisy.

We must cultivate a fair and generous attitude towards the opinions and attachments of others. In the field of psychology attention is directed less to mind-in-general and more to minds-in-particular. More and more it has come to be realized that no two persons are alike. Each is uniquely adjusted to his or her environment. I was tempted to write that each is adjusted *or maladjusted* to his or her environment, but this is not necessary, for what is popularly regarded in any society as maladjustment is but the manner in which some persons adjust to their environment. Perhaps it would be more accurate to say that each is uniquely adjusting to his or her environment, for adjustment is a continuous process. None of us is exactly what we were last week or last year or ten years ago. Such an insight is of enormous importance in the context of thinking for life.

Perhaps the hardest thing to cultivate is a sympathetic understanding of the needs of other persons. It is fairly easy to achieve a detached respect for human personality in general, or even an academic interest in the problem of individuality, but to be sensitive to our neighbour's needs demands a high degree of personal involvement.

Sometimes the minister's concern to maintain theological consistency may lead him to make an incorrect assessment of the needs of others. He must guard against viewing all persons alike and adopting one line of approach to all problems; otherwise he can easily miss the real issues. How often have people sought the advice of others supposedly more experienced only to turn away feeling that their real problems had not been met.

5. *Dedication.*   Dedication is an overworked word in some quarters, and dedicated athletes, dedicated cricketers, even dedicated spin bowlers are sometimes in the news. Yet in other realms too little is heard about dedication, though man in society cannot live without it. Certainly the minister cannot carry on his work without dedication. To dedicate oneself is to lay oneself open to all the demands of one's life and work, and this is the essence of ministry as service.

6. *Compassion and Integrity.*   I place these two together, for what is needed for successful ministry is a blending of the two. There is a danger in compassion alone, for it might impel us in subtle ways to seek to manipulate the other person for his own good. This would be as reprehensible in the ministry as it would be in any other walk of life. What is needed is compassion tempered by integrity. Compassion implies a truly sympathetic understanding and appreciation of what the other person is in himself; and integrity means doing everything possible to preserve the other person's dignity. To maintain one's own integrity and the integrity of others is something to be highly prized in the ministry, as in the case of the parishioner who said of his minister: "I trust that man. He speaks to me frankly but treats me as a responsible human being."

Pastoral care is not paternalism: its essence is service. Any theory of ministry must be developed in the light of "servant" theology and in the context of the concept of the "Servant Church". The Christian minister today finds himself in a rapidly changing world, in which many are consciously aware of the lack of direction and are looking hopefully for some guidance from somewhere. He stands alongside trained workers in the other helping professions as a servant of the people.

2

Psychology and Religion
The Minister as Interpreter

"Psychology", said an old lady, "is just plain common sense." And she was right. At least, it is common sense even if it is not always plain! One wit described psychology as "the science which tells you what you already know in language you can't understand". There is an element of truth in that also.

The functions of psychology are to discover, analyse, and describe the mental processes which stimulate and govern the activities of individuals and groups. It investigates the what, the how, and the why of behaviour. It asks "What?" concerning activity—What does this or that person do in such and such circumstances? It asks "How?" concerning processes—How does he carry out his actions? How are his actions influenced by circumstances? It asks "Why?" concerning motives—Why does he do this or that? By what is he motivated in his actions?

In essence, therefore, psychology is a descriptive science concerned with the mental processes manifested in behaviour. Indeed, modern psychology could almost be defined as the science of the study of behaviour. An illustration is perhaps of value:

Mr X is married to a woman of strong personality and aggressive manner. She rules the household "with a rod of iron", and makes his life at home a misery. He finds that, for the sake of peace, he must adjust to the domestic situation, so he plays the role of a meek, submissive husband. But when he is in the office in his place of business he becomes a different man. He bullies the members of his staff and seems full of the sense of his own importance. He declares that in all things he is right and regards other people as fools. He makes life in the office as unbearable for others as his own is for himself at home.

His wife regards him as "soft"; his typist thinks him a brute and gives him a week's notice; his partner considers him pig-headed and threatens to dissolve the partnership. Some of his business acquaintances who are not so close to him and therefore do not suffer from his tantrums regard him mildly as a "case".

Why is he so pig-headed in business? What makes him so unbearable? The psychologist might use the word *compensation*. At home Mr X is subjected to humiliation by submission to a stronger personality, and deep down in his mind he is wounded by the humiliation and resents it. So he seeks a compensation; he is determined to be master in some realm, so he vents his feelings on his employees and close business associates. Behind his strange behaviour is the mental process of the demand for *compensation*. Often the struggle for superiority is but an effort to compensate for a deeply felt—often a wholly unconscious—inferiority. We shall say more about the unconscious mind later on; but this simple illustration sheds light on the What? the How? and the Why? of psychological inquiry, and shows what is meant by "the mental processes which stimulate and govern the activities of individuals".

Religious experiences and activities are forms of human behaviour and as such are worthy of and amenable to scientific study.

Religion stems from, or at any rate relates to, at least three fundamental human needs: 1. The need for freedom—the need for autonomy; 2. The need for affection—the need to love and to be loved; and 3. The need for significance—the need for wholeness, the need "to be the best that I can be". In very simple language—I need to be myself—I need to be somebody's—I need to be somebody.

If it is asked, "What is religion and what are its prime functions?" there is no simple answer. Elsewhere I have suggested that broadly speaking religion consists of a configuration of beliefs and a set of ideals, an attitude of acceptance of and dedication to those beliefs and ideals, and a mode of behaviour consistent with the acceptance of those beliefs and ideals and dominated by them.

In an attempt to reduce the scope of the definition religion may be said to be man's sense or awareness of sacredness and meaning; or it may be more simply defined as the philosophy by which a man lives.

Religion has suffered both at the hands of its exponents and at the hands of its opponents. Some exponents have tried to formularize it to such a degree that it is robbed of its essential spontaneity and life, whilst some opponents simply have not understood it for what it is. By and large it has been the religions of the world that have been concerned with the spiritual life of man and its development and have provided the impetus for man's highest aspirations.

The best judge of the value of religion is not the philosopher, not the sociologist, not the psychologist, not even the theologian, but the saint. The sages and seers and saints have not all been neurotic persons seeking the solace of a fool's paradise. Some may have been, but not all. Many were—and many are today—sane, mature, integrated persons who live in the real world of affairs on a high level of personal achievement and fulfilment in the service of their fellow men. They are persons who really have come to terms with life.

Religion is concerned with the major problems of human existence:

The problem of the meaning of life.
The problem of the nature of ultimate reality.
The problem of man's position in and relation to the universe.
The problem of evil, especially the problem of pain.
The problem of the good life, the problem of behaviour, of right and wrong.
The problem of man's relation to man.
The problem of death and of the issues of death.

It cannot be urged that there is universal agreement among the great religions of the world on these matters, or even that there is agreement between different groups within each of the various religious systems of mankind; but it can be affirmed that in the main all have these basic concerns.

It is because religion deals with such human problems that psychology can and ought to be used as an instrument of its illumination and elucidation.

To look at the matter more closely, it is clear that these are precisely the points at which human beings break down and where the contribution of the minister is most needed. Individuals break down when life has lost its meaning or when a meaning for life has never been discovered; they break down in the face of ultimate responsibility; they break down under the strain of physical crises; they break down under the burden of guilt feeling; they break down in their relationships with other persons; they break down in the face of death and in the hour of bereavement.

Religion seeks to aid man in his search for truth concerning himself and his world, in his concern to know the end purpose of all things, and in his striving to be at one with reality. Ideally religion aids man by providing a framework for life, a way of adjustment to life and a means to fullness of life.

The word "ideally" needs to be stressed, for the religious experience of some persons does not appear to bring about such healthy results. This is due in large measure to the fact that religious experience is a human experience—the experience of human persons. The human element is sometimes overlooked or minimized by those who view religion primarily in its supernatural context.

Religious experience does not differ from other forms of human experience. The thought processes involved and the emotions evoked are precisely those that appear in other forms of human activity. Religious faith, hope, love, joy, fear, and all other emotions connected with the religious life are not special emotions experienced only within the context of the religious life; they are ordinary emotions such as are experienced in a number of human contexts, but in this case they are stimulated by religious ideas or concepts and are directed towards and experienced in relation to religious aims or ends or objects.

There are three possible ways of using psychology in the study of religion. One is to use it destructively and to imagine that by coming to understand the human aspects of religious development or the "mechanics" of the religious life, such as the processes by which religious beliefs are formulated, religion has been explained and therefore explained away.

Another possible use of psychology in this connection is to examine the intensities and frequency of occurrence of religious attitudes, beliefs, and practices, and to use the data to "prove" their truth or validity.

Neither of these uses of psychology is legitimate, and their findings cannot be regarded as unequivocal. The only legitimate way to use psychology in the study of religion is to apply its techniques in the same way as they would be applied to the study of any other form of human behaviour and to interpret the findings accordingly. All one can do is to be as objective as possible, always admitting that unconscious factors are operative and that since a man's basic psychology is involved, it inevitably colours his judgements. I began my studies with theology and have moved into psychology without forsaking theology, and in the process have come to appreciate how and why so many different theological views are possible and why some folk have come to reject theology altogether. Whatever else is reflected in these pages, I hope that my own understanding of and sympathy with many points of view will be apparent.

Modern psychology is rightly concerned with man's bodily functions or physiological processes. All this is of great value, but it has its dangers. It is possible to be so absorbed with physiological data as to come to regard man almost as a machine, and this could lead to a soulless psychology, a psychology without the psyche, which might better be termed a *somology*. When mental or extra-sensory data are taken into account a vitalistic conception of man seems necessary. Man is a machine. That is true. Yet he is more. He is a self-conscious being, a person who thinks and feels and acts. It is only on the assumption that man is more than his bodily functions and when human intelligence is taken into account that the study of religious experience, or any other kind of experience for that matter, can proceed.

By derivation *psych*ology is *soul*ology, and as such it has much to say to the minister for his work.

Although it is not the prime purpose of psychology to judge the truth or otherwise of beliefs held by individuals or groups being studied, questions involving judgements inevitably arise in the course of investigation. The psychologist or the minister who could not see the appropriateness or inappropriateness of certain religious concepts, or who could not judge their value or otherwise for natural, healthy human development, would be singularly lacking in the insight expected of him. Thus he would have something to say about the quality of the nature of the concepts behind the behaviour or the experience he is studying, whether in an academic setting or in a counselling situation. A religion based on love, for example, will always be deemed preferable, from the point of view of healthy human development, to a religion based on fear. The psychological study of religion cannot help revealing pathological elements or morbid states within the psyche when they are present, for this is one of its areas of concern.

Psychology can be of enormous help to those engaged in the work of the ministry. It is not the gospel or a substitute for the gospel, but it provides insights for the understanding and ministering of the gospel.

Psychotherapy and the cure (or care) of souls are both alike and different. Psychotherapy is something more and something less than the cure of souls. It is more in that it requires a greater degree of expert knowledge and professional skill than most ministers possess. It is less than the cure of souls in that it is not normally related to the individual's finding a religious or spiritual orientation to life.

Psychology can aid the minister in various ways. It can help him to understand his own and other people's experience. Frequently, especially in the pastoral setting, the minister is called upon to be an interpreter of human experience. "What is happening to me? Why should this happen to me?" a person in distress will sometimes plead; and the minister has to do his best to interpret life to the inquirer.

An important point for the practical ministry is this. An adequate knowledge of psychological principles would enable the minister to detect when a particular person's problem is beyond his own competence to deal with. The importance of this cannot be exaggerated. Every minister should have sufficient knowledge to enable him to read the signs of those forms of mental disturbance which are the province of the medical profession. When he meets this kind of trouble the most "pastoral" thing he can do is to refrain from meddling with problems beyond his skill and to refer the sufferer for medical treatment.

An adequate knowledge of psychology can likewise aid the minister in his teaching and preaching. He is called upon to minister to persons of different ages and at different stages of their development. He has to instruct children, adolescents, and adults. No one can be expert with people of all ages, yet he has to minister to them all.

As teacher and preacher the minister has to apply his message to persons in varying states of need—belief and doubt, moral and psychological crisis, grief and anguish, sickness and death. The more he knows of the human psyche and its needs the better able he is to help.

A knowledge of psychology can help the minister in his special work of caring—that is, in his work as pastor. In the pastoral encounter he comes face to face with those who feel that they have committed the unpardonable sin; those who can forgive others but who find it impossible to forgive themselves; those who carry heavy loads of real or imagined sorrow or suffering; those who fear life; those who fear death. Once again, the more he knows, so much the more he can help.

Today, with more understanding between members of the helping professions and with increasing opportunities for ministers to have some amount of training in psychology and clinical methods, a new form of ministry should be possible for some clergy. They would have to be professionally trained in psychology and perhaps in psychotherapy in addition to being educated in theology and its related subjects; but, given goodwill all round, there is no reason why selected ministers adequately trained should not find a special place alongside others in the helping professions on a professional basis.

It may be a long time before this ideal is fully realized. In the meantime those responsible for the future training of ministers could prepare the way by seeing that all ordinands are given some amount of training in psychology and clinical experience, and by planning to make provision for those who show a special aptitude for this work to be given the opportunity to receive the appropriate training.

Sometimes when I have been lecturing to ministers on the value of psychology for pastoral work and have illustrated it by reference to cases of counselling, a minister has approached me afterwards and said: "How is it that you come across these people, or these people come to you? I never meet them in my work!" And my answer has always been the same: "You do meet them, but perhaps you have not learnt to recognize them."

Ministers are interpreters of experience, and they need all the help that psychology can give them.

3

Psychology Today
The Minister as Learner

When the Psalmist asked: "What is man?" he raised a question which has engaged philosophers and theologians in many ages. In the last hundred years or so the question has become a scientific one.

The psychological study of man in its modern phase began in the last few decades of the nineteenth century. It is usual to summarize its progress in terms of the contributions made by the various "schools" of psychology as they emerged. It is not necessary to survey the whole field, but there are some formulations of the past and some developments in progress in psychological theory at the present time that are of special interest to those engaged in the work of the ministry.

Depth psychology is one such formulation. This includes Psychoanalysis (Sigmund Freud) and the psychological systems which stem from it, especially Analytical Psychology (Carl G. Jung) and Individual Psychology (Alfred Adler). It is termed Depth Psychology because of its concern with the deeper, unconscious aspects of mental life.

For Freud, much human behaviour is determined by unconscious motives and "forgotten" memories of the past. Symptoms of physical disease often have their origin in the mind; and much overt behaviour is but the outward expression of internal, unconscious conflicts. Many of our conscious attitudes are so determined, and even our highest and noblest aspirations may be due to hidden motives beyond our ken.

Freud postulated the existence of three strata or levels of mental life—the Conscious, the Subconscious (sometimes referred to as the foreconscious or the preconscious), and the Unconscious. In general parlance these are conceptualized on the analogy of depth.

Accordingly, the *conscious* level is the level of *awareness*. It has been called the organ of perception. A man is aware of his immediate environment, of happenings around him. He is aware of what he is thinking or feeling or doing at any given moment, and this level of awareness is designated the conscious level of mind, or the conscious mind.

The *subconscious* (or foreconscious or preconscious) is that level of mental life which is "just below" the level of consciousness. It stores up memories which might be said to be "forgotten" but which can be recalled at will. As you read this book it is doubtful whether you are thinking of the subject about to be raised, but if you were asked: "Where did you spend your last holiday?" you would immediately be able to recall not only general impressions of your last vacation but particular incidents in detail. These are memories which, so to speak, are "out of mind", but which are stored up and can be recalled voluntarily or by association through something that is happening at the present moment to remind you of them. Thus we speak of the subconscious level of mind or the subconscious mind.

The *unconscious* level, on the analogy of depth, lies beneath the area of the subconscious and is the burial-place, as it were, of past experiences. It retains those memories of the past which cannot be recalled at will. It is an area of the mind that is totally unknown to the individual—hence the term "unconscious", which implies inaccessibility rather than lack of activity. The unconscious mind is very active. It is not unconscious; it is the individual who is unconscious of the content of this area of his mind.

There is a sense in which we never really "forget" anything. It is still in the mind even if we cannot recall it. But nature has a helpful way of dealing with memories which are of an unpalatable nature, memories which would cause pain or embarrassment, or which would hinder healthy normal development. It represses them. That is, it relegates them to the unconscious so that we no longer "remember" them. No one is able at will to recall memories so repressed, though they can be brought to light and are indeed exposed by psychoanalysis, hypnosis, or some other form of psychological aid such as drug treatment.

How memories are relegated to the unconscious is a nice academic question. Freud regarded repression as one of the defence mechanisms adopted unconsciously by a person in order to protect himself against painful feelings associated with memories of unpleasant experiences. Later writers of the so-called Neo-Freudian school have modified this conception. Harry Stack Sullivan preferred to speak of "selective inattention", the individual by-passing, as it were, the events or confrontations which he wishes to forget, whilst others are banished from consciousness by "disassociation".

The niceties of the discussion need not detain us. But what is of interest is the fact that memories relegated to the unconscious are not really forgotten; they are active as motivating impulses to behaviour.

Jung developed his theories and methods beyond those of Freud. Jung postulated an even deeper level of unconsciousness, namely, the *Collective Unconscious* or the Race Mind. This represents those elements in the unconscious mind which are derived from the experience of the race. He spoke of archetypes or archetypal images which colour traditional ways of thinking and feeling and acting.

Adler, famous for his exposition of the inferiority complex, made an important contribution from the point of view of our study in his emphasis on people as individual, separate persons, each with his own personal memory, with his own unique personality resulting from his own unique constitution and social adjustment, and with his own life-programme to fulfil.

To trace more recent developments in depth psychology—and there have been developments and also divergencies from some of the original conceptions—would take us beyond the purpose of this chapter and too far outside the scope of our special interest. Suffice it to say that the basic concepts of unconscious motivation and the need for personal insight into one's own attitudes remain constant. The very principles and prejudices by which we live are often due in large measure to unconscious motives and factors. By a process known as "rationalization" we can, and frequently do, find excuses and reasons for our behaviour and for the views we hold; but this does not rule out the possibility of unconscious motivation or minimize its power.

Great strides have been made in recent years in the study of body-mind functions. It seems better to speak of body-mind functions rather than the more usual body-mind relationship, so as to avoid a dichotomy.

The influence of mental on physical conditions and of physical on mental conditions is well known. Psycho-physical or psycho-somatic phenomena (as they are some-times called) are the common study of psychologist and physician.

On the physical side much progress has been made in the treatment of mental illness by physical means. Cortical undercutting, the severance of nerve fibres in the brain, in cases of obsessive depression and compulsive states fre-quently relieves the symptoms and produces marked changes in personality. Shock treatment (Electric Convulsion Therapy) used in cases of depression and other illnesses, and the various drug and hormone treatments are further examples of the treatment of mental states by physical means.

Then there is the new and developing science of Psycho-genetics, the study of inherited bodily features as deter-minants of behaviour. The literature currently appearing in the study of physical traits and behaviour patterns makes fascinating reading.

On the mental side it is well known that states of mind affect physical health. The mere suggestion of illness to some persons is sufficient to bring about symptoms of physical disorder, whilst cheerful-mindness can often help a person to overcome some of the effects of physical disease. Unconscious mental conflicts can be converted into almost any form of bodily disability. It is the work of psychotherapy to help the patient to health by understanding and facing the emotional disturbances which frequently manifest themselves in physical forms.

There is no need to turn to specialized medicine for examples of psychosomatic functions. They are observable everywhere.

Some students in college decided to play a prank on one of their number. On a certain day his friends were to suggest to him that he was looking unwell. The first one to meet him in the morning said: "Hello! Are you all right? You don't look well." Others quickly followed, saying: "What is the matter with you?" "Have you had a bad night?" "Have you been sick?" "You look awful." As the morning wore on he began to feel poorly, and by mid-day was in bed feeling very sorry for himself.

On the other hand, a very old lady underwent a major operation. She made a remarkable recovery, and the surgeon who performed the operation congratulated her and told her that it was the calm manner in which she faced the crisis that had brought her through.

I knew a man who had been an alcoholic for years past. The craving for alcohol was so great that he could not live without it. One night, against his wish, he was almost literally dragged by friends into a down-town Mission Hall. What he heard there brought back memories of his Sunday School days. He was converted then and there—and from that moment the physical craving for alcohol left him never to return.

Existential Psychology has been gaining momentum during the last few years, first on the Continent of Europe and more recently in the United States of America and in Britain.

In general, existential psychology emphasizes (a) the importance of the existing person in his emergence or becoming, his achievement of selfhood; and (b) the immediacy of experience in the here and now. From the days of Freud emphasis has, rightly, been placed upon the past—especially upon past traumatic experiences—for later life and development. But sometimes there has been a tendency to overlook the importance of the present. The deterministic element has sometimes been exaggerated. To say that a man is what he is because of what his parents did or did not do for him in early childhood is, of course, true; but to imply that the result of his parents' attitudes is inevitable and that he is in no way responsible for what he is, is an exaggeration. It is against such an exaggeration that existential psychology protests.

Existential psychology brings will and decision into focus. In a helpful essay Professor Rollo May writes:

> A central core of modern man's "neurosis" is the under-mining of his experience of himself as responsible, the sapping of his willing and decision. And this lack of will is much more than merely an ethical problem: modern man so often has the conviction that even if he *did* exert his "will" and capacity for decision, they would not make any difference anyway.... The existentialists' central proclamation is this: No matter how great the forces victimizing the human being, man has the capacity to *know* that he is being victimized, and thus to influence in some way how he will relate to his fate. There is never lost that kernel of the power to take some stand, to make some decision, no matter how minute. This is why they hold that man's existence consists, in the last analysis, of his freedom.... Tillich phrased it beautifully... "Man becomes truly human only at the moment of decision".[2]

There is, of course, much more at stake. Existential psychology includes a number of insights from different writers who may loosely or more exactly be called exis-tentialists, each with his own emphasis or emphases. It covers the whole field of psychology in its various branches. Existential psychology is not a formalized system in any sense. It is a developing attitude and an ongoing approach to the understanding of man and his problems. Once again, the importance of the individual is basic.

A point of immediate interest to ministers is the exis-tential concept of the person-to-person encounter. In their various situations the parent and the child, the teacher and the pupil, the counsellor and the counselled are persons relating to one another in a unique situation—a situation in which each has something to give and something to gain, and in which each is in the process of *becoming*. In other words, it brings to light the dynamic element in every human encounter. In the case of the parent, the teacher, the counsellor (and, we might add, the minister) it is not merely a wise person giving advice or imparting knowledge to a less wise person; rather, it is two persons experiencing together, and both developing in the process.

Here is a valuable insight for the ministry. In so many day-to-day contacts people do not really meet; their relationships are superficial. A disappointed church member remarked after an interview she had sought with her minister: "Oh! yes, he listened to me but he did not hear me." She was really saying more than she said, and he did not hear her. He may have had a clear idea of the general circumstances of his parishioner's problem, and perhaps gave good advice; but he had not met *her*, and she knew it.

A form of existential psychology that calls for special mention is Logotherapy which has become known as "the Third Viennese School of Psychotherapy" (its predecessors being the Freudian and Adlerian Schools). Its founder and chief exponent is Professor Viktor E. Frankl, Psychiatrist and Head of the Neurological Department of the Poliklinic Hospital, Vienna.

Under the Nazi regime Dr Frankl was arrested and incarcerated in two of the worst of the concentration camps, Auschwitz and Dachau. At the time of his arrest he was already a medical doctor in high standing. During the years of his imprisonment he kept himself sane by studying his own reactions and the reactions of his fellow prisoners to their deprivations and suffering. He tells the story in his book, *From Deathcamp to Existentialism*, and his fuller work, *Man's Search for Meaning*.

In the deathcamps Dr Frankl found that those for whom life had lost its meaning more easily succumbed to their fate and lost heart than those for whom life still had a meaning and who, in other circumstances, would have had much for which to live. The key, he found, was *meaning*. This confirmed for him a conviction which was already formulating from his psychiatric work, and so he developed his philosophy of healing. As its name implies, it is a therapy based on the concept of meaning (Logos = meaning). A few sentences taken from *Man's Search for Meaning* will illustrate his general outlook:

> Logotherapy, in comparison with psychoanalysis, is a method less *retrospective* and less *introspective*. Logotherapy focuses rather on the future, that is to say, on the assignments and meanings to be fulfilled by the patient in his future.

> In logotherapy the patient is actually confronted with and reoriented toward the meaning of his life.

> Logotherapy ... focuses on the meaning of human existence as well as on man's search for such a meaning.

> The will to meaning is in most people *fact*, not *faith*.

> I think the meaning of our existence is not invented by ourselves, but rather detected.

> One should not search for an abstract meaning of life. Everyone has his own specific vocation or mission in life to carry out a concrete assignment which demands fulfilment. Therein he cannot be replaced, nor can his life be repeated. Thus, everyone's task is as unique as his specific opportunity to implement it.

> As each situation in life represents a challenge to man and presents a problem for him to solve, the question of the meaning of life may actually be reversed. Ultimately, man should not ask what the meaning of his life is, but rather he must recognize that it is *he* who is asked. In a word, each man is questioned by life; and he can only answer to life by *answering for* his own life; to life he can only respond by being responsible. Thus, logotherapy sees in responsibleness the very essence of human existence.

Here is a practical philosophy of life as well as a way of healing. Dr Frankl sees man as living in three dimensions:

the somatic, the mental, and the spiritual. In Dr Frankl's use of the term, *spiritual* does not have a specifically religious connotation; it means, rather, *that which makes man human.*

Dr Frankl recognizes the uniqueness, or as he calls it the singularity, of every human person, and the need for each to seek the values that can give meaning for his existence. He speaks openly of the meaning of life, the meaning of love, the meaning of work, the meaning of suffering, and the meaning of death. Every life has its own specific meaning for the individual if only he can find it; and every life has its unique opportunities to decide upon its aims and manner of fulfilment.

Another approach of current interest is described in a book entitled *Reality Therapy: A New Approach to Psychiatry*, by William Glasser.[3] Dr Glasser and his collaborator Dr G. L. Harrington, working through psychiatric problems with young delinquents and with other mentally disturbed persons, have in recent years arrived at a pattern of treatment which they call Reality Therapy and which appears to be having an encouragingly high rate of success. In brief, the theory behind the treatment consists in what has been called "a psychiatric version of the three R's, namely, reality, responsibility, and right-and-wrong". They view their patients as persons who are out of touch with reality, who have lost (or who have never had) a sense of responsibility and are therefore living irresponsibly. They work on the assumption that only as their patients learn to live responsibly will they begin to seek worthy ends and thus fulfil their real needs. This, of course, is only a tiny glimpse into the system, but its relevance for our study can clearly be seen.

An approach which calls for some amount of elaboration is that known as Psychosynthesis. It owes its inspiration to Professor Roberto Assagioli of Florence. For over fifty years Professor Assagioli has been practising various methods of psychotherapy, and his theory and techniques are the fruits of his long and vast experience. As the word implies, psychosynthesis is a drawing together of various strands of thought. It aims at synthesis. It sees the value of unifying all knowledge for the benefit of mankind. More especially it seeks a synthesis in relation to psychotherapeutic theories and methods, and aims in its therapy at the synthesis within the individual of all the separate and separative elements of the psyche.

Like other forms of existential psychology, psychosynthesis takes as its starting-point *the self from within*. It sees the person as growing, developing, and in the process of actualizing many latent potentialities. It emphasizes the importance of meaning, that is, what each person brings to life and gives to life and expects from life. It recognizes the importance of values for life in its fullness. It takes into consideration such aspects of human living as choices, decisions, responsibilities, and motivations which determine choices and decisions; and it has in its philosophy a place for suffering. Its emphasis is on the future, with full recognition of its dynamic role in the present; for the future is in the present.

Dr Assagioli goes further than some other existential psychologists. In his scheme of things he lays great stress on *will* as "an essential function of the self and as the necessary source or origin of all choices, decisions, engagements". He is concerned with what he terms "the direct experience of the self, of pure *self-awareness*". At its highest this is similar to that which would be described as "spiritual experience" in religious terms. Indeed, the highest synthesis is, for Dr Assagioli, spiritual. It would take us too deeply into the technicalities of the theory to enlarge upon this here; but what is of significance to us is the fact that this dimension of human experience, so close to that which we are concerned with as ministers, is receiving scientific investigation at the present time.

Dr Assagioli is interested in the positive, creative, joyous experiences of life as well as in the tragic and painful ones which for so long have seemed to be the main concern of psychiatry. In his therapy Dr Assagioli has learned to use active techniques in assisting his patients to a new and "higher" synthesis within.

The late Professor Abraham H. Maslow, of Brandeis University, and other American scholars have been developing a form of existential psychology which has come to be known as Humanistic Psychology. Like the other therapies mentioned above, its concern is with the development of the human psyche in its higher reaches.

Indeed, the term Transpersonal Psychology is being used, and extensive, penetrating studies are proceeding in the fields of spiritual self-knowledge, peak experiences, ecstasy, mystical experience, transcendence of the self, bliss, awe, wonder.

To give these developments a single name, perhaps they could be subsumed under the general term *Value Psychology* or *Psychology of Values*. It must not be thought that they are religious movements. They are not. They are scientific developments and their insights stem from clinical research and professional experience in psychology and psychiatry. Nevertheless they have an obvious bearing upon the psychological understanding of religious experience, and anyone approaching the scientific study of religion would do well to take note of them.

In short, the inner life of man is open to scrutiny. Spatial language is always inadequate, for it is only figurative; yet it is useful if taken in a symbolic sense. Thus it might be said that the study of religion and religious experience is the study of *Height Psychology*; or, in the language of Professor Assagioli, the study of the Higher Unconscious; and in the language of the New Testament, the life of the spirit.

Religion is in the world, and, with all its differences in emphasis and belief and with all its manifold forms of expression, is still a dominating influence in the lives of multitudes of persons.

Religion cannot be ignored: it needs to be understood. Only through understanding, indeed, can its purpose be known, and only by probing to its depths—or to its heights

—can its value for mankind be assessed. The minister is its interpreter. But he is ever a learner, and there is much to guide him in these latest developments in psychological theory.

4

Religious Development The Minister as Teacher

Religion, psychologically speaking, is a human sentiment, and as such is subject to growth. A sentiment is defined as an emotional disposition, a master motive, which controls the life-impulses so as to direct them to purposeful ends. When religion is the ultimate guiding principle in a person's life it can be called the dominating sentiment.

The religious sentiment develops in the same way as other human sentiments. It is the product of many interacting forces and factors. The three most powerful influences are sometimes described as nature, nurture, and experience. Nature consists of all inherited traits which make a person what he is by birth. Nurture has reference to upbringing. Experience covers all those fortuitous circumstances that surround the individual from the beginning to the end of life.

The saying that religion is caught, not taught, is one of those half-truths which, if taken literally distort rather than clarify matters. The fact is that religion is both taught and caught. The child learns it from his elders but has to internalize it, identify with it and make it his own if it is to become the dominating influence of his life.

It is possible to trace the stages in the religious development of persons just as other forms of human development can be traced. It is possible also to discover points of arrested growth. Both development and arrested development are matters of consequence to the minister in his teaching office; it is therefore fitting to give serious attention to them, for they are all part of the human experience of persons as they respond to the formative influences within their environment.

A stimulus is an object or event which causes a person to react in some way or other. The response is the reaction thus aroused. The event or object stimulates the response—or, more accurately, stimulates the observer to make a response. In psychological text-books sometimes the abbreviations SR or S–R are used to describe the process of stimulus-response.

Some stimuli evoke a response of fear. A large vicious dog in angry mood would be one such stimulus. Some stimuli evoke a response of love—for example, an act of kindness or generosity, a display of sympathy, a word or gesture of tenderness, to mention but a few. Other situations will arouse responses of joy or jealousy or concern and many other emotions.

A man being cruel to a child would stimulate feelings of disgust and anger in the onlooker who might feel the impulse actively to intervene to restrain the man. That would be his response. The sight of the man being cruel to the child would set up a chain of reactions involving: (*a*) A train of thought (he would think how cruel the man is and how much the child must be suffering); (*b*) Deep emotions (disgust and anger); and (*c*) Purposive action (the going forward to restrain the man). In other words, thought, feeling, and will would be stirred within him even though he might feel he had acted on impulse.

Personal factors enter the S–R situation. The individual making the response (referred to as the "Organism" in psychological language) has to be considered. All persons do not react in the same way to the same stimuli; and the same person will sometimes react to the same stimulus in different ways at different times and in different circumstances. Indeed, the individual person or organism (for whom the letter "O" is used in the formula) is often the governing factor. What disgusts you may not disgust me; and what disgusts you today may not disgust you in ten years' time. So the formula needs to be enlarged to make it more accurate, and written as S–O–R. The stimulus plus the factors contributed by the organism equal the response. Or more briefly: $S + O = R$.

This is a valuable insight for the study of religion, for it provides a framework for the understanding of personal religious development. Let us illustrate it by an example:

Four children in the same family, A, B, C, and D, are nurtured in the atmosphere of a devout Protestant home. A continues in adult life in the same tradition as his parents; B becomes a Roman Catholic; C breaks away from all religious observance and becomes an Agnostic; D develops a wide interest in the study of world religions and seriously leans towards Buddhism. These are facts of experience, but the questions arise: What did each child receive from his environment? How did he react to it? Why did he react as he did? The answers lie in our understanding of the individual person—the Organism in our formula.

There are three typical reactive tendencies—imitation, sympathy, and suggestion. Imitation is the tendency to act as we see others acting. Sympathy is the tendency to feel as we perceive others are feeling. Suggestion is the tendency to accept and to act upon ideas, beliefs, and opinions conveyed by the words, attitudes, and actions of others. Suggestion is especially effective when it emanates from one who is greatly admired, or who is in a position of authority, or whose example is reinforced by some other form of prestige or status value.

A child is very open to the influences around him. He naturally tends to imitate and to feel and to believe in ways that secure his attachment to those he loves and upon whom he is dependent.

Children used to be taught (and I suppose some still are taught) to sing: "Jesus loves me, this I know, for the Bible tells me so." Whereas, as someone has rightly remarked, it would be nearer to the facts of the situation if they were to sing: "Jesus loves me, this I know, for my mummy tells me so."

Thought, feeling, and will are points of contact between the individual and the outside world. In the realm of thought (that is, in the process of the development of opinions and beliefs) he is open to suggestion from others. Thus, a growing child dependent upon his parents and loving them, tends to hold their opinions and beliefs long before he has any rational grounds for doing so. In the realm of feeling he tends to adopt the emotional attitudes, likes and dislikes of those he admires or loves. Sympathy means feeling with others and is a prime factor in social development. In the realm of willing or acting he tends to imitate the behaviour of those he admires or loves.

These are potent factors in human development in general and therefore, of course, in religious development. The more one studies the human factors in religious development the more evident it becomes that basically, and in the first stages at least, religious development is the result of environmental pressures involving suggestion and producing responses of sympathy and imitation.

There is, however, another factor to be considered, and that is the element of contrasuggestibility. Some persons, far from being open to suggestion, are contrasuggestible—that is, they tend to react in the opposite way to that which is suggested. This is sometimes observable in a curious manner in small group relationships. *A* will always oppose what *B* suggests, not because *B* is always wrong, but because of an underlying and unrecognized antipathy between *A* and *B*. Some folk seem to be habitually contrasuggestible —they are always "agin the government", and their constant opposition to, and their nagging criticism of, everyone and everything becomes for others an irritating and annoying trait.

It is sometimes said that youth is the age of contrasuggestion; and this poses a nice problem for parents and ministers and teachers and whoever else might be responsible for the religious education of young people. Some young folk react against religious and moral training if the pressures of the training are too strong or if the demands are too stringent. A well-meaning adult can unwittingly call forth a contrary response by over pressure or too stringent demands.

Through our five senses—sight, hearing, smell, taste, touch—we are continually receiving impressions from our environment. Sensation, or the process of sensing, is the psychological link in the S–O–R process. "Sensible objects" are objects which can be sensed; or, to put it in slightly different form, they are objects which may be known and experienced through the senses.

Perception is the accompaniment of sensation. It is the process whereby a person apprehends the existence of sensible objects as distinct entities.

A percept always has reference to some particular object —for example, this desk, this book, that man, that tree, that cat. We build up our knowledge of our environment by thus apprehending or perceiving individual objects or situations in this way.

A concept, on the other hand, is an object of thought rather than an object of sense. It is either a thought-construction involving the idea of the general nature of a number of similar entities of a particular kind, or it is an abstract general notion.

We may illustrate the thought-construction of a number of objects in the following way: As a percept the word "tree" means this tree or that tree, for a percept has reference to some object having its own position in space or in time. As a concept, "tree" is an ideational notion, a general idea, made up of our experience of many trees. From our knowledge or experience of trees we might draw a "tree", but it would be quite unlike any particular tree we had ever seen. We have in our minds (as we say rather loosely) a general idea of "tree" or "trees". Examples of a concept as an abstract notion would be: Justice, wisdom, righteousness, fairness, goodness, evil.

An infant's world is a world of percepts—a conglomeration of separate objects. As he experiences a variety of objects of the same class, the growing child moves from the perceptual to the conceptual stage of thinking.

A baby is born into a home where there is a large black cat with a bushy tail. This is referred to in the home as "Kitty". As the infant develops and is able to understand a few words, the word Kitty conveys the image of this particular large black cat. As his experience widens he sees a tabby cat, a marmalade cat, a white cat, a piebald cat; big cats, small cats, sleek cats, lean cats—until he develops a concept or thought-construction involving the idea of the general nature of a number of cats. From the percept Kitty he has developed an ideational notion of "kitty-ness" which can be applied to this, that, and the other kitty.

At some stage he may see a small four-footed animal and call it Kitty; but he is corrected. That is not a kitty; it is a dog or doggie. From there he has to build up a concept of "dogginess", and this is different from his concept of "kittyness". From perceiving the object itself, he moves towards an appreciation of the qualities which make the object what it is. In essence, growth from infantile to mature thinking is the process of development from perceptual to conceptual modes of thought.

Imagination functions in two ways. On the one hand, it means imaging, or the reviving of an image of past perceptual experience. On the other hand it means the creation of a new image, an image of what might be. Imagination in both these ways plays a large part in the process of mental development and in the development of character. The Wise Man of the Book of Proverbs says: "As one thinks in his heart, so is he."

Reason follows conceptual thinking and stems from perception, attention, and imagination. Language is the instrument of reasoning, for ideas are conveyed by words. Reasoning is sometimes defined as the process of thought involving the drawing of inferences or conclusions, or of solving particular problems by the application of general principles.

The reasoning of children is simple and in the main related to practical problems. Through a variety of experiences or through the repetition of a particular experience they perceive, pay attention, and imagine. Thus they conclude that this or that action produces this or that result. This act is "good" whilst that act is "naughty"; but at first good and naughty carry no ethical quality. A good action is one which brings parental approbation, whilst a naughty action is one which is followed by parental disapproval. Here is simple reasoning, the logic of childhood. As the child grows older and more informed he will come, as a natural development, to pay attention to ideas conveyed by words, until eventually he arrives at ethical concepts involved in such words as "good" and "evil". As he grows in knowledge and experience so his powers of reflection and reasoning will increase.

Conceptual thinking and reasoning lead to belief. Belief is that attitude of mind which involves the recognition and acceptance of something as real or true. Belief is an important topic in the study of religion. Belief is not a simple matter; it is a complex of ideational elements coloured by upbringing, education, experience, temperamental make-up, and other factors in an individual's personal psychology.

Religious belief involves certain positive affective and volitional attitudes. Belief is thus closely related to faith; but normally religious belief is understood more particularly in its rather restricted aspect of intellectual content. It cannot, however, be limited to intellectual content; my own strong conviction in the matter, supported by considerable experimental data, is that the emotional element plays a much greater part in the formulation of beliefs than many believers realize. Undoubtedly the most potent factor in the formulation of religious beliefs is upbringing. And the same is true of disbelief. The tendency to believe or to disbelieve depends to a significant degree upon whether the individual, especially in the formative years of his life, is encouraged to believe or not to believe; though, of course, he makes his own unique response to what he is taught in order to make it his own. Another simple formula may be useful:

Let "A" represent the innate, often indefinable, qualities with which the child is endowed at birth. These are the raw data of the self. Let "B" represent those characteristics which he acquires through the interplay of environmental and personal forces from the formative years of early childhood and onwards into maturity. And let "C" represent the developing personality as seen in his beliefs and attitudes. Then it may be said that A + B = C. What he is in himself plus his reactions to what he is taught and encouraged to be are the human factors which determine the form and quality of his responses to life.

The psychological approach to a study of the religion of childhood is in keeping with the modern attitude to child study in general. The normal processes of development observable in a child should be looked for in his religious development.

All the evidence seems to point to these facts concerning the nature of a normal child's religion if he has one: (1) It is emotionally toned and emotionally centred; (2) It is largely a matter of imitation, the child tending to develop the religious habits he sees in his elders; and (3) It is stimulated, sustained, and coloured by the child's own imagination.

In the religious training of children example is always better than precept, and love is more powerful than any other influence. I once heard a clergyman say that as a child he used to be taken regularly to church by his mother and father. On entering their pew his parents would kneel down to pray silently, and the clergyman said that as a little boy the sight of his parents praying always filled him with an emotion which then he could not have put into words. Now he thinks that what he felt was something like this: "I depend on them, and they depend on God."

It is important for adults to remember that children think in childish ways, and they cannot be expected to mean what adults mean when they use religious terminology. When children are still at the stage of perceptual thinking they build up their religious ideas accordingly. A little boy, out after dark for the first time one evening, and seeing the moon, asked his father: "Daddy, does God rest his feet on the moon? Is that how he stays up in heaven?" Another little boy asked his mother: "Why do we keep going to Church?" "We go to meet the Lord Jesus," replied his mother. Some weeks later on the way home from

Church the child looked puzzled and remarked: "Mummy, we keep going to Church to see the Lord Jesus, but I have never seen him there." A little girl, told that we go to Church to hear the Word of God, astonished her parents by revealing casually that she thought the vicar was God delivering his Word from the pulpit.

We could go on multiplying examples, and anyone who has had close contact with young children in their religious development could add other stories of their own. The explanation is that the child is thinking in percepts. The child imagines heaven as a place, and God as a person—greater and more powerful than other persons, of course, but nevertheless a person like the people he knows. Add to this fact the power of the child's imagination, and he is in a theological world all his own. Therefore he sometimes misunderstands when adults teach in concepts or by analogy. I remember a boy in an Approved School. He had attended a religious service where the speaker had referred to the fatherhood of God. The boy remarked, "If God's a farver 'e aint like my old man. My old man's in jug for robbery with violence."

All this raises questions for religious education, questions which the minister ought to face in his work as teacher of the Faith. In my own studies I have given attention to the problems which arise in the religious thinking of children, and here would like to deal with three typical problems— fear, doubt, and guilt.

Careful investigation has led to the conclusion that many children brought up in a religious atmosphere are subject to fears of one sort or another, especially where the discipline is strict and the standards of conduct demanded are high. Such fears are conditioned partly by the kind of religious teaching the child has received and partly by the vividness of his own imagination. Many children never mention their fears to their parents or other adults around them, and even the most attentive parents can be quite unaware of the terrors which frighten their children. This is not extravagant language. My investigations have uncovered childhood fears which had never been revealed to other persons—fears connected with death and the life to come; fears of judgement; fears of "being left behind" on the Last Day; fears of not meeting parents and loved ones in heaven. These fears obviously reflect a certain kind of teaching, but the fault does not always lie with the parent or teacher. The adult in all good faith uses language which conveys certain ideas to himself, but the child tends to embellish that language with ideas appropriate to his own stage of development; and the result is gross distortion. The two sets of ideas—those of the adult and those of the child—may be very different from one another without the adult realizing it.

In my case histories I have records of vivid dreams experienced in childhood—dreams amounting to nightmares causing intense fear. A small child dreamed regularly of being left behind when her parents were being taken up to heaven. Another dreamed that he was being pushed away by a big hand because he was not fit to meet Jesus. These are not rare or specially chosen examples; they are typical of many that have been told to me.

Something else that a great many adults never suspect is that their children entertain serious religious doubts, simple in their childish way but often profound in their implications for the children themselves. Here are a few examples:

A child's prayers centre around concrete objects and factual situations. A prayer is not answered, and the child begins to wonder why. He may not reveal his problem to an adult, but he begins to doubt.

It is sometimes said that a child has a keen sense of justice. This is outraged by the manner in which God appears to be managing (or, rather, mismanaging) his world. A small boy said: "It isn't fair that Granny should be ill and have to stay in bed all day every day", when he contemplated the problem of his bed-ridden grandmother. A little girl thought: "It isn't fair that God should punish Satan. Satan can't help it: I want Satan to be made better." Here are the beginnings of a problem which in later life might be recognized as the problem of evil.

Then there are doubts associated with the child's growing knowledge. At first he imagines that everyone believes and behaves as his parents do. Their beliefs are his presuppositions, and their behaviour is his norm. But he comes to discover that all people do not believe and behave as he has been brought up to do. And when he sees (a) inconsistencies in the lives of his mentors and of other adults who make a profession of religious belief, and (b) the attractiveness and likeableness of adults who not only do not believe, but who openly reject the beliefs of his mentors, then the question of the validity of what he has been taught as normative presses itself upon him.

Guilt is another problem. Some adults tend to read adult significance into the manifestations of a child's sense of guilt. Conscience is not fully developed in a child. In the earliest stages of a child's self-conscious awareness he is innocent of wrong-doing and cannot differentiate between morally right and morally wrong actions. His standard of judgement is that of expediency. He is a "good" boy when he pleases his parents; he is a "naughty" boy when he displeases them. And for a long time "good" and "naughty" have very human, natural meanings for him. He is a "good boy" when he answers the call of nature at the right time and in the right place; he is a "naughty boy" when he "has an accident" and performs his natural functions without warning. Thus he learns to adopt the standards of his environment.

Nevertheless, children do feel a sense of guilt in a religious context even in quite early years, due mainly to the type of instruction received plus the child's own temperamental nature and imagination. Just as he feels sometimes that he has displeased his parents and fears that he will be punished, so in a childlike way he may feel that he has displeased God and that God is likely to punish him. Thus guilt and fear are intermingled. A little girl prayed every night (secretly and without telling her parents) that she might die in the night. The reason? She had in her prayers confessed her sins and asked God's forgiveness, and she wanted to die in a forgiven state and feared to live till the next day when she knew she would be sure to do something to displease God.

Adults need to be very careful in what they teach children concerning sin and forgiveness; in fact, many adults still live at the childish level in this matter themselves.

Three typical human developments appear to influence the religious outlook of the adolescent. There are, alas, many adolescents who do not manifest these traits because for one reason or another they are not maturing properly. In describing the following tendencies the young people in mind are those who are coming to maturity inspired by religious ideals.

One such typical form of development is in the sphere of intellectual awareness. The young person begins to think conceptually, in terms of ideas and ideals. His intellectual horizon is enlarged. Things he once took for granted now have to be sorted and tested and proved. This is the age of questioning.

Then there is an emergent socializing tendency which is typical of puberty. Coincident with the growth of sexual awareness the adolescent passes from the stage of habitual self-reference to that of object-reference, when he sets his affections on objects external to himself and looks for persons to love and ideals to follow. It is noteworthy that adolescence is the age at which most religious conversions occur, especially around the years 15 and 16.

Finally, there is a growing sense of responsibility. This includes a developing awareness of obligation and duty and a willingness to accept responsibility. The young person begins to feel responsible towards himself, towards other persons, and towards life in general. He looks for meaning and purpose in life. Moral virtues take on a new and deeper significance, sentiments are consciously focused, and thus the ethical self emerges.

Such developments bring their own difficulties, and the problems of adolescent religion are worthy of close attention. As problems they are as numerous and as diverse as the persons who experience them, but for purposes of analysis they can conveniently be categorized as intellectual, moral, and practical.

Intellectual problems vary according to the education, ability, and temperament of the individual, but they are classifiable as scientific, theological, and personal problems.

Serious difficulties arise, especially amongst more educated adolescents, as a result of being trained in school in the scientific method. Many religiously-inclined adolescents battle within over the apparent contradictions between science and religion. Some manage to solve their problems by coming to a maturer view of religion; some contrive (with varying degrees of success) to keep scientific and religious ideas in separate mental compartments; but many fail to make any adjustment and, on grounds of intellectual integrity, forsake the religious way of thinking in favour of the scientific. Many of these may continue to be inspired by religious impulses (though they might prefer to call them idealistic or altruistic impulses), but no longer subscribe to the Church's dogmas and are not to be found amongst its active members.

Theological difficulties are closely related to and follow naturally upon questions raised by the scientific method in general. In my studies of the problems of religious adolescents every one of the Church's main dogmas has been questioned and rejected by someone. One interesting finding is that a growing number of thoughtful young persons are more interested in the religion *of* Jesus (i.e. the religion by which he lived) than in the religious or theological ideas *about* Jesus with which they think the Church has been too greatly concerned. Many young persons with serious theological difficulties are not irreligious; they are deeply interested in religion and welcome discussion in a frank and open manner.

Personal problems arise from the other two types of problem just mentioned, for after all it is the individual who is involved whatever the problem. Particularly some adolescents feel personally threatened when they face the question of choosing between one set of ideas or tenets and another—especially when the choice may involve the rejection of a set of ideas which previously they have sincerely held, or when they know that their choice may conflict with the known views of their parents and mentors.

Moral problems are numerous. In times past many young people experienced feelings of guilt in relation to sex impulses. Some young people still do pass through this phase especially when they have been brought up in an atmosphere where sex is regarded as something impure—and there are still homes where this is so. Today young people are faced with problems as they look out on life. One great problem is the question of the meaning of life. Many of our young folk are weighed down by the burden of the apparent meaninglessness of existence; and many thoughtful young persons are searching for meaning.

Others are concerned with problems on a world scale— social justice, the treatment of delinquency, problems in relation to life and suffering and death; birth control; extramarital sex; drugs; abortion as a social problem; how to curtail the population explosion; the use of nuclear power; war and peace; the implications of man's entry into space. These are some of the moral problems confronting modern youth and to which they are seeking an answer. Some are asking: "Can religion suggest any answers?"

Practical problems arise from the others and often appear to be related to the growing sense of responsibility noted above. The youth whose dominating sentiments are religiously inspired naturally sees all life in relation to these central aims and ideals. Often he is faced with such questions as: What shall I do with my life? What is to be my life's mission? Work, leisure, money, relationships, ambitions—all are seen as part of a whole, to be woven into a life-pattern for which he is personally responsible. These are personal problems which have to be individually solved.

Mature religion is characterized by just those traits which characterize maturity in general; but three such traits particularly related to the religious life are worthy of note.

One is ability to view religious ideas objectively and to hold truths in tension. Some time ago I was shown a printed programme advertising a series of lectures arranged in defence of a certain narrow theological position, and the remark was made to me: "Look at the names of the speakers, and look at their degrees. They are all university men. Nobody can say that we are obscurantists." But obscurantism is not a matter of education; it is an attitude. An otherwise educated person can be obscurantist in the matter of religion. Obscurantism in an adult is an anachronism, a sign of immaturity. Objectivity in outlook, even accompanied by a certain amount of healthy agnosticism, is sometimes demanded of the mature adult.

Another characteristic of maturity is tolerance, and this will be seen as charity in the appreciation of other people's points of view. "I am holier than thou", or "I am right and you are wrong" are hardly attitudes of maturity, but unfortunately they are not infrequent amongst religiously-minded persons.

A third mark of maturity is willingness to think again on religious matters and to experiment for the sake of those who come after. This is not to condone an iconoclastic attitude to the past, but it does demand a responsible concern for the needs of others brought up in new ways of thinking now and in the future. In the process of spiritual growth everyone inevitably, and to a certain degree quite unconsciously, comes to accept as essential ideas and forms of belief and habits which, looked at objectively, are incidental and not essential to the Faith we hold. Indeed, the essence of growth is change, and what once was held as essential may come to be seen as incidental, and vice versa. The mature person recognizes this.

The path to maturity, however, is not always an easy or direct one. The following are some likely problems that can be encountered on the way.

In the realm of belief there is the tension which can be epitomized as: *Adult knowledge* versus *adolescent or even childish ideas of religion*. Theologically speaking, some adults live in perpetual adolescence. But sooner or later difficulties arise for the adult who tries to live his religious life at adolescent levels of understanding.

In the realm of experience there is the tension which can

be epitomized as: *The reality principle* versus *adolescent hopes and expectations*. Young men see visions; old men dream dreams. Adolescent expectation and adult experience do not always match, and the adult comes to realize that life does not always work out as anticipated. He has therefore to learn to take a philosophical view of the situation, otherwise he is faced with a perpetual problem.

In the realm of practical everyday living there is the tension which can be epitomized as: *Adult responsibility* versus *adolescent ideals*. Since adolescent hopes and expectations are not always matched by adult experience, the question which sometimes faces the adult is: "What is the use of living by the ideals of my youth?" This is largely a problem of moral stability and integrity, a problem of being in conflict with one's own inner convictions.

In all these areas of the religious life—in belief, in experience, and in matters of practical concern—the adult can be expected to show poise, breadth of outlook and understanding, as well as conviction and a sense of dedication, for these are signs of maturity.

Healthy life in whatever realm entails growth, progress, development towards maturity. So in the religious life this should be the norm. What are the obstacles which hinder so many from reaching spiritual maturity? They are numerous, but some at least are fairly common:

Some young people (as we have noted) experience serious intellectual problems, and these are often made more difficult by our educational system. In the school classroom it is frequently assumed or at least implied that science and the scientific method are the only intellectually respectable pursuits and that no thoughtful person trained in science can continue to be religious. Now this is a matter of intellectual integrity. In current agnostic literature it is sometimes implied and sometimes openly declared that religion closes people's minds. No one who knows the facts will deny that it sometimes does precisely this; but it is equally true that the so-called scientific method can close the mind to the appreciation of aesthetic and value judgements. Let us be fair. It may be necessary in our modern society for education to be concerned with packing children's minds with facts; but it is just as important for them to learn to cope with life, to judge the value of ideas and ideals, and to know the secrets of healthy human relationships. Young people have to face problems; it is a serious matter if teachers (many of whom are themselves still on the road to maturity) are unable or unwilling to allow young persons in their care to face their problems without bias.

Some young people in religious circles are not allowed to develop in their own way. There was the girl who went to university to study science. She had been brought up in a conservatively religious home. At university problems which had begun at school were intensified. She found herself moving out into a much more liberal position. She met friends who belonged to a Christian denomination other than that in which she had been nurtured and where more liberal views were entertained. For some time she kept her questionings to herself, but one day during vacation she began to tell her parents about her new friends and said that she felt she wanted to join their denomination. They immediately opposed her, and with some vehemence. They saw this as quite clearly "the work of the devil" and did all they could to keep her within what they conceived as the true fold. Little did they realize what they were doing. The very mention of the devil at that stage of her thinking was a psychological blunder of the first magnitude, for the girl no longer believed in the devil! And they never knew the depths of the anguish they caused their daughter by such a censorious attitude. This is only one story, but it would be possible to tell others like it. Parents, ministers, and teachers need to be careful lest they hinder rather than help their charges towards spiritual maturity.

Sometimes in religious circles artificial problems are created for young persons by the overbearing demands of adults or of the religious in-group to which they belong. Everyone, whether religious or not, has an area of suppression the content and extent of which vary from person to person. By an area of suppression I mean that we all choose not to do some things in order to do other things. An athlete will forgo tobacco and alcohol in order to achieve success in the field—this is his area of suppression. The standards by which we live are both negative and positive. We decide to deny ourselves in one area in order to achieve a higher standard. In some religious circles, however, unnecessary taboos are imposed; young people are expected to conform to patterns that are unnaturally rigid, and as a result artificial guilt feelings are engendered and spiritual development is hindered.

Sometimes the problem is simply that of the failure of the spiritual life of the individual to keep pace with the natural, normal growth into adolescence and adulthood; for it is clear that adolescent religion is not adequate for adult life.

To the question: "What is the secret of spiritual growth?" the usual answer might be something like: "By prayer and sacrament, by reading (especially Bible reading) and meditation, and by fellowship." Here, however, the more situational aspect of the problem is in view.

In the process of development from childhood religion to adult religion there are both losses and gains. A child's religion is emotionally centred, it develops by imitation, and is coloured by imagination. Emotionality, imitation, and imagination are good in their way but must not be allowed to dominate in adult life. They need to be replaced by stability, insight, knowledge.

The pattern of growth is likely to be along the following lines: From simple credulity to some amount of intellectual understanding; from intellectual understanding to personal acceptance and commitment; from personal commitment to self-realization; from self-realization to personal autonomy, integrity, and responsibility.

The final secret of personal growth is to lay hold on life itself and on what can be conceived as its highest purpose. Practical psychology and the wisdom of the ages say to man seeking life: "Know thyself—accept thyself—be thyself". Religion adds, both as a challenge and as a means of personal fulfilment: "Give thyself".

5

Psychology of Faith
The Minister as Guide

Faith is one of the elusive words of the Christian religion. It is rich in content yet difficult to define especially from the point of view of psychology, for psychology imposes its own restrictions.

The theologian is able to bring to his study of faith certain presuppositions. He may assume, for instance, that faith is a gift of God, or that it is the measure of a man's response to the revelation of God, or that it is the means whereby man comes to the knowledge of spiritual reality and of truths which could not otherwise be discovered.

The psychologist cannot begin his inquiry with any such presuppositions. All he can do, to be true to his science, is to look at faith as a form of human behaviour, or, rather, as a phase of mental activity manifested in behaviour, and try to interpret it accordingly. Such concepts as God, or revelation, or discoverable spiritual truths are outside his frame of reference. He has no way of assessing their validity or their meaning.

However, to confine discussion to a descriptive analysis of faith so as to satisfy the demands of strict psychological discipline would be inadequate for the immediate purposes of this study. Something more difficult therefore must be attempted, namely, a psychological study of faith, but of faith as a means whereby persons are brought, or at least feel themselves to be brought, to an apprehension of spiritual truth which inspires them to live as Christians. By this means it is hoped to use psychology as a practical aid to pastoral understanding.

In his *Dictionary of Psychology* Professor James Drever defined psychology as

> the branch of biological science which studies the pheno-
> mena of conscious life, in their origin, development, and
> manifestations, and employing such methods as are avail-
> able and applicable to the particular field of study or
> particular problem with which the individual scientist
> is engaged.[4]

Faith he defined as

> acceptance of a belief without conclusive or logical evi-
> dence, and usually accompanied, influenced, or even de-
> termined by emotion.[5]

These definitions are of value because they are psychological definitions, or, more accurately, the definitions of a
psychologist. But they do not go far enough to meet the
requirements of the present study; it is therefore important to penetrate further into their meaning.

The very word psychology is full of significance. *Psyche*
in its root meaning denotes soul, or breath, or life, or the
life-principle, or mind, the seat of desire, reason, and will.
Drever defines psyche as "originally the principle of life,
but used generally as equivalent to mentality, or as a substitute for mind or soul".

Faith can be defined more fully in the course of the argu-
ment, but here it may be noted that faith is more than
belief and it involves more than mere emotion in its expression. It follows that Drever's definition, useful as it is in its
setting, is by no means adequate for the full understanding
of religious faith. It resembles too closely the schoolboy's
definition that faith is trying to believe what you know is
not true.

Each branch of psychological study employs methods of
research available and applicable to the particular field and
the specific problem under review. There are various forms
and manifestations of faith; but since it is religious faith—
and particularly Christian faith—which is under considera-

tion, the appropriate method of approach is through the biblical record.

In English versions of the New Testament the word *pistis* is generally translated "faith" whilst the cognate verb, *pisteuo*, is generally rendered "believe". *Pistis* has a number of meanings, some of which can be expressed as intellectual assent, fidelity, confidence, or trust.

But to appreciate the New Testament meaning of faith it is necessary to turn back to the Old Testament. There faith means not so much belief in a dogmatic sense, but rather faithfulness (i.e. trustworthiness); confidence, such as trust in God, or in his word, or in his messenger. God is a God of faithfulness, or a faithful God; whilst faithfulness is a desirable trait in men. Faith as confidence or trust involves man in casting himself upon God. The just lives by his faith—or by his faithfulness, his stability. By faith or steadfastness he is established.

Although belief is not the primary meaning of faith in the Old Testament, yet belief is necessarily one of the elements of faith. The righteous man believes in the faithfulness of God, puts his trust in God, and is thereby established. *Pistis* is used in the Septuagint, so it is an easy transition from the Old Testament concept of faithfulness, confidence, and trust to the New Testament concept of faith as belief. But it is noteworthy that in the New Testament faith is belief *in*, not mainly belief *that* or belief *about*. To believe in God is to rest assured in him.

In short, the biblical idea of faith denotes: (*a*) a character trait—steadfastness, stability, faithfulness, fidelity to the pledged word; and (*b*) an attitude of confidence, trust, and belief. Thus as a personality characteristic and as an habitual attitude faith may be said to be an aspect of maturity, almost equivalent to integrity and perhaps even to wholeness which is an important biblical theme.

Religious faith is not different in essence from faith in other human contexts, such as faith in another person or faith in the practicability of some of the projects men plan. What is special about it is its setting. It is stimulated in the context of and directed in relation to specifically religious ideas or ends or objects.

In the light of present-day psychological thinking it would be inappropriate to speak of a religious instinct or faculty as something apart from the rest of man's experience. Today the emphasis is on the unity of the self, and life is seen in the whole; it is therefore fitting to view a person's religious ideas, feelings, and impulses as part of the total pattern of his experience of life.

Today it would be more accurate to speak of a person's religious orientation—that is, his dispositions, his attitudes, and his commitment to religious ideas and ideals. In this extended sense faith could equal orientation. Only when such a comprehensive standpoint is established is it safe to begin to analyse faith.

Religious faith as observed in the experiences of individual persons relates and answers to a variety of deeply-felt needs, impulses, and aspirations: awe, sometimes tinged with fear; a sense of curiosity and inquiry; the impulse to explore the mysterious; desire for insight and understanding; a quest for life; negative self-feeling, sometimes associated with the awareness of finiteness, sometimes expressed in feelings of inferiority and in attitudes of humility; and positive self-feeling experienced as a sense of human dignity, the desire for the higher life, a sense of call, mystical experience, dedication to a high vocation or a noble cause.

These are not universal. They are not present in every experience of faith, but they are found in varying intensities in different persons and in the same persons at different times. The point is that faith involves a wide range of human propensities.

In its fullest expression faith is a function of the whole psyche. If for purposes of analysis faith is taken to denote belief, confidence, and trust, it can be said to correspond to the three main activities of the human psyche—thought, feeling, and will. In other words, faith is an intellectual, an emotional, and a volitional response on the part of an individual to another person or to an idea. Thought, feeling, and will are not disparate, unrelated activities; they are interwoven in any response pattern. Faith properly so called involves the whole psyche.

To speak of *the* faith (for example, the Christian Faith) is to think not only or mainly of its formularies, its organized systems of belief; it is necessary to bear in mind attitudes also and the responses which they evoke. *The faith* is a derivative term; it represents that which is believed, experienced, trusted, and acted upon.

Thus, in the New Testament mention is made of those whose faith is sound; those who have erred from the faith; those who contend for the faith; those who have no faith, or who have little faith. Christians are exhorted to live by faith, to walk by faith, and are said to be justified and sanctified by faith. A person can be said to have faith or to manifest faith when he shows himself confident, trustful, steadfast, stable in the midst of strain and stress.

Faith as an activity of the psyche has both a subject and an object. The self is the subject, the idea or thing or person in which or in whom the self reposes trust is the object. Psychologically speaking, faith must have an object even if that object is the self. To mature and to live in the fullest sense a man must have faith—faith in himself, faith in others, faith in life itself. Religion, rightly conceived, can help a person to have faith in himself, though it does not leave him there, for its avowed function is to inspire him to attitudes of reliance, trust, and confidence in something or someone outside and beyond the confines of his own self.

Religious faith is inspired and sustained by the conviction that there is a unity, a consistency, a fundamental congruity at the heart of things.

To the religiously-minded person life is not capricious, but constant, sure, securely rooted, and grounded in certainty. Life has a meaning for the religious person, and all its vicissitudes are but opportunities for him to discover that meaning in new ways. And this holds good even when appearances are against him. He says with the writer of the Epistle to the Hebrews: "Now faith is the assurance of things hoped for, the conviction of things not seen"; or, as in Dr Weymouth's rendering: "Now faith is a confident assurance of that for which we hope, a conviction of the reality of things we do not see."

Religious faith in the sense of confidence, steadfastness, and trust is founded upon the fundamental belief that there is stability at the heart of things, that life is not altogether capricious or contingent, that there is meaning in human existence. The Christian will wish to articulate this belief by affirming that his faith is built upon the certainty of the changelessness of God. This is the faith of Israel; it is the faith of the Church—"I the LORD do not change." "I am who I am." "Jesus Christ is the same yesterday and today and for ever." These are some of the affirmations of faith, and the faithful can confidently sing:

> Change and decay in all around I see:
> O thou who changest not, abide with me.

Both theologically and psychologically speaking, faith is not complete in itself. St Paul reasons soundly in 1 Corinthians 13 when he links faith with hope and love. Faith implies an upward look. It must have an object. Hope implies an onward look. It must have an outcome. It is closely linked with faith. It is the outcome and development of faith. "I believe, therefore I hope, I trust." Love implies an outward look. It must have an outlet. Love is the expression of faith and hope.

Religious faith is dependent upon and often determined by very human factors. Upbringing, education, fortuitous experience, temperament, social status, and other non-theological factors all contribute to the presence or absence of faith and to the specific content of faith where faith is present. The Hindu and the Christian will have different views of God, and possibly different attitudes to God, in the first place from the fact of having been nurtured in different cultures. Add to this fact differences in types of education, differences in temperament and all the other psychological differences between them, and it is no wonder that they differ so radically in their religious outlook.

And this analysis applies also to differences between Christians of diverse traditions—as between Catholic, Orthodox, and Protestant. When theological differences are examined against the background of personality, education, and culture it becomes evident that they are to a significant degree psychologically and culturally determined.

For some persons religious faith is vindicated by experience. There is a saying to the effect that faith begins in an experiment and ends in an experience. In such a case the psyche makes its commitment and in the process comes to be. As our Lord said, the man who loses his life finds it, and he who would save his life is in danger of losing it. "Abraham believed God, and it was reckoned to him as righteousness." Moses "endured as seeing him who is invisible".

There is in vindicated faith an element of triumphant optimism, an assurance (that is, an inward feeling of certitude) that in the end faith will give place to sight. "Now we see in a mirror dimly, but then face to face. Now I know in part; then I shall understand fully, even as I have been fully understood."

The analysis given above is as factual as it can be on the data available. But the data themselves are by no means unequivocal and in fact are capable of more than one interpretation.

It is for example sometimes assumed that faith is natural to man and may be expected of everyone. But such an assumption is dubious. Faith is not the only reaction of the human psyche to religious stimuli. Sometimes a person reacts negatively, such a negative reaction resulting in religious doubt.

To define faith in terms of belief, confidence, and trust might suggest that doubt should be defined, at least roughly and superficially, as unbelief, lack of confidence, lack of trust. But faith and doubt are closely associated as personality traits. Sometimes doubt is an element of faith, or at least its precursor. And just as faith involves thought, feeling, and will, so doubt may arise from or relate to intellectual, emotional, or practical problems.

I once heard it said that there are three kinds of doubt. There is doubt with a sneer in it. For example, the mockers at the Cross: "If you are the Son of God, come down from the Cross . . . and we will believe." There is doubt with fear in it, as the fear of Thomas: "Unless I see . . . I will not believe." He was almost afraid to believe. Then there is doubt with a tear in it—the doubt of the father of the sick child: "I believe; help my unbelief."

This is a nice, simple analysis, not without its value for homiletical purposes; but it is not adequate for a real understanding of doubt. It is so necessary for the minister to understand doubt that it will be relevant to give further attention to the psychology of unbelief or doubt.

For some persons unbelief is easier than faith. Faith appears to create so many problems that life is less complicated for them if they can discard it. In other cases unbelief is due to a genuine inability to accept what is taught as true in religion.

A man who had read much, listened to sermons and lectures, and engaged in serious dialogue with exponents of several forms of Christianity in the end became so confused that he gave up trying to believe. He used to say: "These good men (the preachers and lecturers and others with whom he discussed religion) are all sincere, they all believe in what they say, and they all think that they are right. But they hold such differing views that if one of them is right, then some at least of the others must be wrong. I find it easier not to believe than to believe."

Again, some unbelief is a concomitant of faith. A person who loudly proclaims agnosticism may be very near to faith. There is sometimes an element of doubt or indecision in the most profound attitude of faith. The experiment of faith does not always issue in experience. Faith of itself does not offer the assurance of an experience, and sometimes the experiment involves a conflict between belief and doubt.

This is a very important fact. Mature faith is not being

certain about everything. It is not knowing all the answers to every conceivable question. Rather, it is stability. Maturity does not mean freedom from tension but the ability to live with tensions and to deal with them constructively. So with faith. Faith does not mean freedom from uncertainty but ability to live with uncertainty and to weave it into the pattern of life.

A friend of mine used to say that faith is not walking in the clear light of day, but putting our hand into the hand of God and stepping out with him into the darkness of the unknown.

I would be willing to omit the clause about clasping the hand of God. I would prefer to say simply that faith is stepping out into the unknown; for, when we reach out our hand we cannot always find God, yet life demands that we go forward.

As Martin Buber has pointed out, faith means trusting someone, or acknowledging a thing to be true, "without being able to offer sufficient reasons" for our trust or belief. It is this basic uncertainty, this "not being able to offer sufficient reasons", which makes it faith. Certainty would not be faith. It is also this basic uncertainty that makes doubt a constructive element in triumphant faith.

Surely it was something like this that St John of the Cross was saying when he used the image of the dark night. Faith is not knowledge; it is a journey into the dark unknown.

Some unbelief is a form of escape. When a person fears to face the issues or demands of healthy religion, an easy way out is to feign unbelief. He may rationalize the situation and persuade himself that he genuinely disbelieves, but his rationalization may well be only a further form of escape.

This leads to a consideration of some of the more serious aspects of unbelief. It is certain that some unbelief results from deep unconscious motives. Unbelief may arise from prejudice, or it may be due to a streak of contrasuggestibility in the person's make-up. But some unbelief is definitely pathological. Anyone trained and experienced in counselling at depth will recognize the symptoms of what is sometimes called morbid or obsessional doubt. This may manifest itself in various ways. In ordinary life it may take the form of putting off decisions, delaying actions, apprehension about being committed to anything. In the realm of religion this trait will reveal itself in compulsive doubt.

It would be an over-simplification, and would not be true to experience, to assert that faith always triumphs over doubt. Doubters have been changed, it is true; and sometimes a person who has vacillated for years and feared to be committed to anything religious or otherwise, has become a stable, robust person dedicated to a clearly defined life purpose as a result of a dynamic religious experience such as conversion. But this is not invariably the pattern. Sometimes doubt has to be faced over a long period. Some religious persons, though heartily sincere, are never free from doubt. This is a matter which needs to be sympathetically understood by those who would help others to faith.

That unbelief can be a way of escape has already been noted. But so can faith. In faith there must of necessity be some optimism, some amount of conviction that "all things work together for good to them that love God" or however else we like to express it. But herein lies a danger. Such an attitude can hinder personal growth if it does not spring from healthy motives, for then it could be a retreat into a world of fantasy. To live in the confidence that all things work together for good may be a sign of maturity, but it could be a form of escape; it could be a way of shutting one's eyes to realities and to conflicts which ought to be faced. Confident faith may be the result of psychological freedom, the person having arrived at a healthy stage of autonomy; but it could be due to inner bondage and to fear of achieving self-realization.

Faith may begin by stepping out into the unknown. The element of uncertainty may be a hindrance or an impetus to progress according to the nature of the individual's response. It may be either a stumbling block or a stepping stone according to the use that is made of it.

The question is sometimes asked: "Is there need for faith in a technological age when men are becoming more and

more computer-minded? What room is there left for faith?"
Perhaps the best answer is in the form of a further question: "Can man ever live without faith?" It is of the essence
of life. It lies at the roots of our very self-confidence. If man
is confident that science will eventually be able to explain
all the mysteries of life, that very confidence is faith. Faith
cannot be ignored. The spirit of man, reaching out beyond
the things that are seen, seeking to know more about the
universe in which he lives, will yet have to exercise a measure of faith greater than ever before. And if civilization is
to survive in the process it will be on the basis of faith,
hope, and love.

Faith is not contrary to reason though it is not dependent upon it. Faith and reason are complementary. Faith
is not mere credence. Some knowledge is essential to faith.
In this regard someone once defined faith as "a volitional
surrender to an intellectual conviction".

But human knowledge is limited, although continually
expanding, and it is sometimes possible to apprehend (by
intuition or by faith) what we cannot comprehend (by
knowledge or reason). Sometimes an object of faith can be
authenticated or at least supported by reason though it
could not have been discovered by reason alone. Anselm
went to the heart of the problem when he prayed:

> I do not try, Lord, to penetrate thy Height, for in no
> degree do I match my intellect with it; but I long, in
> some degree, to understand thy Truth, which my heart
> believes and loves; for I seek not to understand, that I
> may believe; but I believe, that I may understand. For,
> for this very reason do I believe, because, unless I believe,
> I shall not understand.[6]

Here are faith and reason blending in experience. This,
however, is not the mental mood today. The attitude of the
new age is: "I doubt in order to understand." The point is
well expressed by Dr Erwin R. Goodenough, Professor
Emeritus of Religion at Yale University. Professor Goodenough writes: "The man of our generation who is in real
trouble is the one who has lost faith in doubting."[7]

This aspect of faith needs to be further explored. Perhaps the message for this age is: "Have faith in the validity of your doubting. Do not try to believe in order to understand. Have faith in your doubting to lead to understanding." It may be that Anselm's attitude will satisfy some persons for a long time to come; it will be their way to faith. But it seems fairly clear that it will not satisfy the majority of our contemporaries or their successors. It may well be that a new approach to faith through doubt is called for, and this is a challenge to the modern minister.

Faith must grow, and for such development the individual person normally needs the experience and support of the group. Ideally the Church with its sacramental life, its bonds of fellowship, and its outreach in mission should be able to meet this need. That it is not doing so in many places is evident. One problem before the Church is how to fulfil its task in this respect.

Faith is stability. Yet stability can all too easily harden into rigidity and bigotry. This is a danger to be avoided by the contemporary Church at all costs.

Faith must never become an end in itself. It must be incarnated in life and deed. Down the ages the call has come to the Church, and never was it more relevant than it is today:

> But be doers of the word, and not hearers only, deceiving yourselves. . . . What does it profit, my brethren, if a man says he has faith but has not works? Can his faith save him? . . . So faith by itself, if it has no works, is dead. But some one will say, "You have faith, and I have works." Show me your faith apart from your works, and I by my works will show you my faith.[8]

The minister who can enter sympathetically into the experiences of faith and doubt will be the ideal guide of the future.

6

Psychology and Theology
The Minister as Theologian

The word theologian is often used too narrowly or is too narrowly applied. In common use it suggests an expertise which the parish minister is not expected to possess. This is a pity, for it tends to make the parish minister feel inferior to the expert. This situation ought not to exist. The working minister who is daily amongst his people is the expert in applied theology—or, at least, he should be. Pastoral theology is applied theology, and this is the province of the parish or church-based minister.

This is an age of theological turmoil, and it seems that the turmoil is partly responsible for the current *malaise* concerning the minister's role.

The *Honest to God* debate, the *Death of God* controversy, and the emergence of the new Radical Theology have created difficulties for some ministers. But in fact they may be seen positively as symptoms of a deeply felt need to examine afresh the meaning of the Christian Faith and to recast it in the face of rapidly changing conditions. Part of the Church's task is to relate its message to the needs of men and women living in an increasingly technological society. And this relating, this presentation of the gospel, is the work of the parish minister, not only or mainly of the theological expert. In this sense every minister is a theologian.

Significant phrases recurring in present discussions are "religionless Christianity", "Christianity (or religion) without dogma", "the secular understanding of religion", "non-transcendental religion", "religion as a way of life rather than as a set of beliefs".

It is evident that there is a wide-spread desire for some sort of religious (or, at any rate, some sort of ideological) framework for life; but, especially amongst young persons, there is a growing impatience with established form and a deepening dissatisfaction with traditional expressions of religious belief and worship.

The revolt of a rising generation is no new phenomenon in the history of mankind, and there is a sense in which every age is an age of transition if not of actual revolution. It is nevertheless arguable that the present age is uniquely so described and that what is found in the realm of religious thought and behaviour is symptomatic of the deeper uncertainty that prevails.

In approaching the problem of theology in the new age there are some points which must be conceded and which call for some amount of discussion. Our theology is set in the theoretical framework of ages that are past, and at least in part is based on intellectual presuppositions which are no longer tenable. This can be illustrated by reference to the following doctrines:

The Trinity.   The history of the development of the doctrine of God as Three-in-One and One-in-Three is a case in point. The theological presuppositions, the philosophical frames of reference, the manner in which the controversies were conducted, and the final credal statements that ensued, are all typical of the first four-and-a-half centuries of the Church. Today, if the doctrine of the Trinity were being formulated the ground of debate, the basic presuppositions, and the resultant form of expression would have to be markedly different.

Original Sin.   The idea of Original Sin as it was first conceived and propounded was based on the belief that Adam and Eve were literally the first parents of all mankind and that the whole race, being seminally in the loins of Adam, was morally damaged by his "fall", and that therefore every person born into the world inherits a corrupt and sinful nature. Obviously, if we were discussing the nature of man and his hereditary traits today we should need a very different set of anthropological and psychological presuppositions.

Atonement. This is the illustration *par excellence*, the perfect example of cultural influences on theological formulations. The various types of atonement theory have frequently reflected the deeply felt needs of the people of the time. The Patristic emphasis on victory and on the work of the Logos, the medieval doctrine of satisfaction and the concept of the work of the God-Man, the Reformation emphasis on Divine Law and its attendant Law-Gospel tension, all reflected current ideas and appealed to the felt needs of the times in which they appeared; just as the more recent concept of Christ as the Man for Others and the emphasis on subjective and moral aspects of atonement have developed side by side with a growing interest in the study of human psychology. And there are some who think that the new study of Sociology and Ecology will demand an exposition of the doctrine of Atonement as at-one-ment and in societary terms with emphasis on unity, as fitting to the needs and mental climate of the new age that is upon us.

Eschatology. The doctrine of the Last Things—Death, Judgement, Heaven and Hell—as originally expounded was based on ideas then current. I need mention only the idea of a three-storeyed universe, with heaven above, earth here, and hell beneath; or the literalness of the suffering of souls in the flames of hell—a belief fervently held, and sometimes even cherished, by the faithful. Many modern preachers find Eschatology a difficult subject to deal with; and certainly no one with even a smattering of modern knowledge could possibly expound the doctrine in its old literal, almost materialistic, form.

The first point to be conceded, then, is that our theology is set in a theoretical framework of ages that are past and that it is based on concepts which are no longer tenable.

The second point which must be conceded follows from the first—we have inherited a theology that is based largely on logic and expressed in propositional form. The creeds, for example, are composed of a series of doctrinal propositions, and the great confessions of Christendom are expansions, or extended expositions in logical sequence, of these original propositions.

There is a value and there is also a danger in propositional statements of doctrine. Their value lies in that they make for clarity; they define categories of belief. The difficulty is that codifying a doctrine tends to limit it; it becomes fixed and stultified. This is one of the factors—apart from considerations of fear and prejudice—which make it difficult to restate doctrine. In the restatement there is an inbuilt tendency to change it, even if this is not fully appreciated at the time. This is inevitable. If a doctrine needs to be restated, then it stands to reason that it needs to be changed either radically or in part.

The problem is evident whenever there is discussion about the revision of creeds. Those who wish to revise them wish to do so because they would like to see some doctrinal statements dropped and others altered to bring them more in line with modern knowledge. Those who oppose revision do so on the ground that they are wary of change. They know that to revise the articles of the creed would inevitably lead to at least a partial and possibly to a radical change of doctrine. Modern churchmen frequently recite the creeds "with mental reservations". This may not be a very satisfactory solution to the problem, but they feel that that is all they can do in the circumstances, since they cannot in all honesty accept the implications of the doctrinal propositions to which they are expected to subscribe.

It might seem that the only satisfactory way to revise the creeds would be to start afresh, to state in modern terms the fundamental tenets of the Faith, to compare these modern statements with the more ancient propositions, and to endeavour to come to some agreed statement from the comparison. But that would be a long-drawn-out process; and, in the nature of the case, since language is constantly changing and new knowledge is continually being acquired, by the time the revision is completed and agreed upon, it would be time to start the process all over again! Such is the tantalizing transitoriness of the value of the propositional form.

There is a third ground for concession. Since the basic doctrines were formulated, whole new systems of thought have developed, and vast new areas of experience have opened for mankind.

Almost everything in the realm of thought is different today from what it was in the centuries during which Christian doctrine was first formulated. Twentieth-century man has a different cosmography, a different cosmogony, a different anthropology, a different view of history. His scientific method is new. Physics, psychology, statistics, automation—these are some of the systems, unknown before, that are influencing man and that will influence him for a long time to come.

The fourth point to be conceded is that, influenced by changes in the structure of society and by changes in popular ways of thinking and acting, the Church has had to change its emphasis and even its doctrines from time to time. Two illustrations must suffice.

The doctrine of Resurrection. It is sometimes asserted today that the Church does not believe in this or that doctrine or in this or that interpretation of a particular doctrine. Thus in regard to the doctrine of the resurrection, it is sometimes said that when in the creed it says, "I believe in . . . the resurrection of the body", it really means "I believe in the survival of personality", or something like that. And it is said that the Church does not believe, or require others to believe, in the literal, physical resurrection of the body.

Now, such statements need to be treated with caution. They can be misleading. The fact is, the Church did once believe in a physical resurrection; and that, in fact, is what the statement in the creed originally meant. Modern churchmen may find it difficult or impossible to subscribe to the doctrine, but it cannot truthfully be said that the Church never did believe in it. And if it is admitted that the Church once did believe in it but that now Christians ought not to be required to do so, then here is an illustration of the point under discussion. To accommodate to modern knowledge, the credal statement has to be either rejected or somehow interpreted. To reject it means to deny a doctrine which once was held. And even to interpret it in a way not intended in the first place is to change it almost to the point of denial.

The other illustration is even more striking, and certainly more prominent in these days. It is the Church's attitude to *family planning*.

In 1908 at the Lambeth Conference the bishops of the Anglican Communion adopted the following resolution:

> The Conference regards with alarm the growing practice of the artificial restriction of the family, and earnestly calls upon all Christian people to discountenance the use of all means of restriction as demoralizing to character and hostile to national welfare.

At the time the members of the Conference were concerned with the diminishing birth-rate amongst English-speaking peoples, but they expressed their concern in theological language. The Report of the Committee appointed to consider and report upon the subject of Marriage Problems contains these words:

> Many causes have been alleged for this decline in the birth-rate: some of these, such as the tendency to marry at a later age than formerly, have no doubt influenced the birth-rate; but it is admitted beyond all power of dispute that it is largely due to the loss of sense of responsibility to God for the fruits of marriage resulting in deliberate avoidance or prevention of child-bearing.

And the Report adds:

> There is the world-danger that the great English-speaking peoples, diminished in number and weakened in moral

force, should commit the crowning infamy of race-suicide, and so fail to fulfil that high destiny to which in the Providence of God they have been manifestly called.[9]

There is no need to comment upon the evident sense of pride and satisfaction at belonging to the English-speaking peoples reflected in the statement. That was over sixty years ago. But the theology behind the statement is of real interest. If language means anything at all, then here were the bishops of the Anglican Communion solemnly affirming, in forceful phraseology and with all the weight of their office behind their statement, that family planning is contrary to the will of God and is due in the long run to the loss of the sense of responsibility to God for the fruits of marriage. In their statement the personal and social evils that are said to result from the practice of family planning are subsidiary to its theological importance as being contrary to the will and order of God.

In later Lambeth Conferences, notably those of 1920 and 1930, the language was modified and certain concessions were made; but in 1958, exactly fifty years after the first pronouncements quoted above, the following words appeared in the Report of the Conference for that year:

The Conference believes that the responsibility for deciding upon the number and frequency of children has been laid by God upon the consciences of parents everywhere: that this planning, in such ways as are mutually acceptable to husband and wife in Christian conscience, is a right and important factor in Christian family life and should be the result of positive choice before God. Such responsible parenthood, built on obedience to all the duties of marriage, requires a wise stewardship of the resources and abilities of the family as well as a thoughtful consideration of the varying population needs and problems of society and the claims of future generations.[10]

Now this is a complete reversal of the former statement. In 1908 the bishops of the Anglican Communion were convinced that "the use of all artificial means of restriction" in family development are "demoralizing to character" and "due to the loss of the sense of responsibility to God for the fruits of marriage". In 1958, the leaders of the same Communion were convinced that family planning is a "responsibility . . . laid by God upon the consciences of parents everywhere". Of course, they were not the same bishops; they were men of a later generation, and they lived in an age when the problem was not that of a diminishing birth-rate but that of a population explosion.

I am not suggesting that the bishops in their respective conferences were not sincere in their pronouncements, and I am not levelling criticism at any of them. I believe that they were genuinely sincere. I am merely using this as an illustration of the fact that doctrines do change from time to time under the influence of social needs and pressures. By 1958 family planning was so widely practised, not only amongst those who professed no religion but also amongst church members, that it had to be recognized. The circumstances were such that the doctrinal emphasis had to change.

If it be suggested that a change of attitude in relation to such a social matter as family planning is not really a change in doctrine, the suggestion must be contested; for the doctrines of Man, of Creation, of Providence, of Moral Accountability, and the Theology of Sex are all involved and some of them have been reversed in the process.

Once these points are conceded—that theology is set in a theoretical framework of ages that are past; that it is restricted by the logical and propositional form in which it has been transmitted within that framework; that since Christian doctrine was first formulated whole new systems of thought have developed and vast new areas of experience have opened for mankind; and that, influenced by changes in the structures of society and by changes in popular ways of thinking and acting, the Church has in fact changed its emphasis and even its doctrines—then there follow three conclusions:

First, attention must be given to the real situation, so that it can be assessed for what it is.

Secondly, it is necessary for the minister to look again

at his doctrinal formularies in the light of the content and exposition of his message. Only thus can theology be made to live and be seen to be relevant to the real situation.

Thirdly, he must be willing to listen to his contemporaries (especially perhaps to his younger contemporaries) in order to understand their needs, and to discover what there is (if anything) in the Gospel to meet their needs. He must stand with his people, not as a superior dispensing remedies for needs which are theirs but not his. Rather, he must acknowledge that their needs are his needs and that together they are looking for the living Word to match their common needs.

The psychological study of religion raises serious questions for theology. It is easy to exaggerate them and to forget that theology has grappled with other questions of a scientific nature before; but there are those who believe that the most serious challenge to Christian thinking today comes from the side of psychology, and the parish minister needs to be aware of them. Briefly, there are four questions which need to be faced.

First, there is the question of the validity of religious experience. The attitude mentioned in chapter two is still widely adopted. When the processes involved in religious experience have been explained they are thought by some to have been explained away. If an individual is what he is, religiously, on account of his background, temperament, and education, and if two persons can believe and experience apparently different things from the same source of training, where is the criterion of validity?

Questions concerning the truths of religious concepts and the validity of religious experience are, of course, in the long run metaphysical questions which must be decided upon philosophical grounds; but they are living issues with many persons, and the parish minister will from time to time be confronted with them.

Secondly, there is the question of the subjective element in dogmatic theology. It is a maxim of theology that religious experience came first and dogmatic formulation followed as an attempt to rationalize the experience. Modern theologians acknowledge the influence of cultural and personal factors in religious belief. But the question is sometimes pressed further: How much of what is regarded as orthodox and necessary in religious belief can be attributed to cultural and personal factors?

Thirdly, there is the question of the uniqueness of the Christian revelation. The comparative study of religions puts Christian belief and experience in a new perspective when combined with the study of religious psychology. This is another living issue for the parish minister in these days when families come from other parts of the world to settle in our parishes and bring with them the traditions and religious insights from their homelands. It is a situation with which many school teachers in Britain are familiar, for in a single class several religious traditions may be represented.

I can recall my early studies in Comparative Religion, as it was then called, when I was still an ordinand and beginning my course in theology. Approaching the study from the point of view of Christian theology and from outside, with no experience of direct contact with persons who professed another faith, I could see the differences between the various faiths about which I read. And at that stage of my own development it was not difficult for me to see the superiority of the kind of Christianity that I had experienced.

Today I see the matter in a different light. For years I have been unable to concur with the view that "the heathen in his blindness bows down to wood and stone". I now know that adherents to other faiths are conditioned and prompted by the same pressures, needs, and impulses as those who worship the Christian God. It is the conceptual elements, the ideational contents, that are different. I am not saying that all religions are of equal value or that the day of the Christian mission is over. What I am saying is that the parish minister needs to consider the matter for his ordinary day-to-day contacts with his people. The question is not an academic one which the parish minister can leave to the expert to discuss.

Fourthly, there is the practical question: What aspects of Christian doctrine need to be emphasized today? What is the "Word" for our age?

As we have mentioned earlier, some of our contemporaries are willing to acknowledge the benefits which accrue from a religious attitude to life, benefits in the realms of morality and of stability of character. But the desire is sometimes expressed for a statement of the Christian Ethic alone. Some would welcome an ethical Christianity divested of its supernaturalism, a guide to living without the appendage of a creed to be believed.

Again, this is no new phenomenon. The Church has been asked this question in ages past; but, like the other questions raised here, this is one that directly affects the work of the ministry at parish level. The question of the relation of behaviour to belief is not one which can be safely left to the experts to decide. The parish minister *is* the expert here. He it is who must bring it home to his people.

Theology is the tool of the parish-based or church-based minister. Pastoral theology is applied theology, and the minister is called to be a pastor-theologian. The experts in theology—the linguist, the church historian, the textual critic, and whoever else may be regarded as having special expertise—all have their place and have their specific contributions to make; but the minister working at parish level has to be the living theologian and interpreter.

The more theological understanding he has the better. I have a friend whose ministry over more than thirty years has taken him to work in several parts of the world and with people of very different background, education, and culture. He has worked with backward children and with University teachers and students, with social misfits and with those who try to help them, and in industry with both workers and management. Of all the ministers I know, it can be said of him that he has ministered to "all sorts and conditions of men". He has kept abreast of developments in the field of theology and in other fields of human endeavour; and recently he remarked to me: "In all the work of the ministry, even amongst the most unlikely folk, I find that I need not less but more theology. The more theology I have the simpler I can make my message."

Existential psychology offers unlimited material for the pastor-theologian, for it is concerned with the peak experiences of life, the discovery of meaning, value judgements, self-actualization, interpersonal encounter, mystical experience, and related topics. All this has to be simplified for practical pastoral purposes, but existential psychology provides a whole range of insights for the pastor with sufficient imagination and human understanding to use them.

Sometimes a minister experiences difficulty in relating his own developing theological understanding to the varying stages of growth which he finds in the persons with whom he is in contact. He may feel that his own thinking is much in advance of theirs, and may find difficulty in expressing himself to them. At other times it is the lay members of his congregation who ask the questions and raise doubts. Frequently however, neither minister nor people are prepared to make an approach to each other on the subject of their doubts, and this can have unfortunate results.

There was in a certain church a minister who was erudite in several disciplines including theology, general science, and psychology. One day a friend remarked: "I wish I were a member of your congregation; I should learn so much, for you have so much to teach." To which the minister replied: "Oh! I never preach on these things. I stick to simplicities. The people of my congregation are people with a very simple faith."

About the same time a member of his congregation, perplexed by questions about religion which he was unable to solve, asked a friend what he should do. "Why not go to your minister?" the friend suggested, "He is a man of great learning and he could help you." "Oh! no," replied the man, "I could not possibly disturb him by asking such questions. You see, our minister is a man with a very simple faith."

Special difficulty is experienced when a minister feels uncertain about his own theological position and has doubts about the Faith he is expected to hold. This is a situation where understanding, compassion, and integrity are essential. The minister has no right to parade his doubts; he must be faithful in declaring that of which he is certain at any time. Yet he has a right, and indeed a responsibility, to discuss difficult questions with his people. When in doubt he must be patient with himself, knowing that his doubts of today may be his certainties of tomorrow and his certainties of today may be his doubts of tomorrow. As Samuel Taylor Coleridge wrote: "Never be afraid of doubt, if only you have the disposition to believe, and doubt in order that you may end in believing the truth."[11]

A wise and learned pastor said to a group of younger ministers: "Whenever I doubt, I pause. I never proclaim my doubts. When I am in doubt I look for those things of which I can be certain, and proclaim them."

The pastor-theologian is able to cope with problems only by approaching them openly and objectively, by being humble enough to view his growing knowledge in perspective, by being patient enough to suspend judgement in the face of uncertainty, and by holding truth in love; in a word, by humility, open-mindedness, and charity.

7

Prayer and Worship
The Minister as Priest

The word "priest" is used here rather loosely. It is not confined to one whose functions are to sacrifice, to mediate, and to absolve, which is the usual definition of priest. It refers to the man of God in his own inner life and in his work of helping others to learn to worship.

It might sound old fashioned to speak of the minister as a man of God. Most of the older textbooks on Pastoralia and Pastoral Theology which I have consulted begin with at least one chapter on the personal religious life of the minister himself. His experience of grace and his manner of life together were regarded as his first equipment. He was to think of himself as the man of God dispensing the means of grace to others, applying what he knew of God to what he knew of the needs of his people.

Today the approach is somewhat different. In the deepest experiences of life the modern minister often feels himself to be a companion of his people, a fellow pilgrim or fellow traveller in the Way. He is trained to help others, of course, and service is of the essence of his calling; but in the cultivation of the life of the spirit, and in its expression in worship, the modern minister must stand with his people, not over them.

On one occasion I delivered a lecture entitled *Religion as inwardly experienced and outwardly expressed,* and at the outset drew attention to the misunderstanding that could arise from its title. It might suggest that there is a clear distinction between inward experience and outward expression, whereas there is no such clear distinction.

Ideally the two are one, the expression being the manifestation of the experience.

Spiritual experience is compounded of knowledge, intuition, and inference. Knowledge may be defined as apprehension, perception, cognition, understanding, familiarity through experience with factual data or with ideas, hence practical skill or wisdom. Technically, the elements of knowledge are: (a) Apprehension, or awareness; (b) Comprehension, or understanding; and (c) Erudition or wisdom, the amassing of a body of information. Much of chapter four on human development can be applied to the growth of knowledge. It develops through sensation, perception, attention, imagination, conception, reasoning, and belief. Religious knowledge is acquired by precisely the same process.

Religion, however, is not only a matter of knowledge. Intuition plays its part, and intuition is to be understood as immediate perception or feeling of conviction experienced without any conscious awareness of the mental processes by which the perception or feeling came. This does not mean that there are no mental processes; merely that the person is not aware of them.

Inference follows from knowledge or from intuitional perception. It is logical or intuitional according to circumstances. It may be a logical conclusion from certain given data, or it may be an intuitional insight or a certain awareness based on previous experience.

A great deal of religious knowledge is of the logical sort, acquired from early upbringing and education. It derives largely from hearsay and is built up by memory, selection, association, the use of mental images, language, and symbolism. The ideational form and content of our beliefs are largely of this sort.

Some religious knowledge is partly logical and partly inferential. Faith as to the unknown future may be based on inference from knowledge and experience from the past. The psalmist had every confidence for the future, for he was able to say: "I have been young, and now am old; yet I have not seen the righteous forsaken or his children begging bread." Experience breeds confidence; but when the saint says that he knows the future is secure he is speaking from knowledge that is partly logical and partly inferential. He looks back and he looks forward. He has experienced the goodness of God in the past; he infers that he can trust God for the future. "Surely goodness and mercy shall follow me all the days of my life; and I shall dwell in the house of the Lord for ever."

Much religious knowledge is necessarily intuitional. But this is true of many other value judgements. It cannot be demonstrated statistically that virtue is its own reward, though one may "know" it to be so. When it is said that a thing is "known" in this sense, this is near to the heart of religious experience.

To depend on logic and statistics for information is to doubt very much whether virtue is its own reward. Virtue led to Socrates' being forced to drink the hemlock; it led Jesus to crucifixion. And the spectacle of the righteous suffering whilst the unrighteous flourished like a green bay tree has been an age-long problem for faith. Yet St Paul could say:

> For this gospel I was appointed a preacher and apostle and teacher, and therefore I suffer as I do. But I am not ashamed, for I know whom I have believed, and I am sure that he is able to guard until that Day what has been entrusted to me.[12]

And:

> Brethren, I do not consider that I have made it my own; but one thing I do, forgetting what lies behind and straining forward to what lies ahead, I press on toward the goal for the prize of the upward call of God in Christ Jesus[13]

In such an experience knowledge goes beyond the bounds of logic and common observation. For the apostle, it has become faith, conviction, assurance. He "knows" in his inmost being.

Under the term experience, aspects of the religious life like mysticism and spiritual intuition might be considered. In the broad sense of the word, mysticism can be used for religious experience in general. There is a sense in which all religious experience is mystical, involving as it does perception of the transcendental.

In its narrower sense, mysticism has reference to a special kind of religious experience involving the participant in the processes of purification, enlightenment, and union with God. In this narrower sense mysticism is, and perhaps always will be, the experience of the few; but anyone whose life is governed by religious ideals is open to experiences which at least in some remote way may be called mystical. A mature religious person may be expected to possess some degree of spiritual intuition.

But these would not be the chief signs of maturity. The chief signs, surely, are those revealed in character and behaviour, in what a person is, and what he does, and how he relates to others in their need.

It is useful to remember the double meaning of the word *character*. It refers to what a man is in himself (his characteristics); but its root meaning is to express in writing (i.e. in written characters), that others may read. Some lines from an unknown author are challenging:

We are writing a gospel, a chapter each day,
　By the things that we do and the things that we say;
Others read what we write, whether worthless or true.
　Say—what is the Gospel According to You?

In his book, *Prayer and its Psychology*,[14] published in 1931, Alexander Hodge wrote: "Prayer is intercourse with an Ideal Being, or Beings, conceived as objectively existent, superior, personal, and responsive." He added: "Prayer, as the central act of religion, is universal, and reflects the forms of human social relationship. As a genuine phenomenon of the psychical life, it presupposes definite psychological conditions and produces definite psychological effects."

Dr Hodge analysed the content of believing prayer-consciousness as: (a) Belief in the existence of an appropriate object of worship; (b) belief in the religious accessibility of that being; and (c) Belief in the possibility of mutual communion between the human and divine.

As a general statement it might be true (a) That prayer implies a consciousness of being, for normally a person's approach to his deity enhances his own self-awareness; (b) That prayer implies a desire to grow in spirit and to be at one with ultimate reality; (c) That prayer issues in a deeper experience of religion in the mind and heart and will of the worshipper.

Today, however, many persons—and not least, some ministers—find prayer difficult. When Alexander Hodge published his book in 1931, he felt that he could call prayer "the central act of religion". It is doubtful whether it is this to many today. Of all religious activities, many people find prayer the most difficult. True, many still "say their prayers"; but there are many otherwise religious persons who have ceased even to do that.

The difficulties are partly intellectual and partly practical. Amongst those who have shared their thoughts with me on the subject are some who cannot help feeling that there is an element of unreality in praying. Some see it as auto-suggestion and wishful thinking. Jesus said: "Whatever you ask in prayer, believe that you receive it, and you will." What is this but auto-suggestion? Or is it "positive thinking"?

Others, especially those who are influenced by the present radical theology, find prayer not only difficult, but quite meaningless. If one thinks of God perceptually and in personal terms, then one can more or less reasonably approach him in humble prayer. But if one cannot perceive him in such terms, then prayer as adoration, praise, and petition ceases to have any meaning. This is a real problem for many today.

In facing the problem, an increasing number of persons are finding new meaning for their spiritual life by the practice of contemplation. The worshipper seeks out a quiet place, relaxes, consciously turns away from distracting thoughts, and dwells for a time upon a single theme—life, love, liberty, peace, reconciliation, power, goodness, justice, wisdom, or any other theme relevant to his life at the time. The psalmist said: "I commune with my heart in the night; I meditate and search my spirit."

Dr F. C. Happold likens this to a journey inwards.[15] It heightens self-awareness, deepens self-understanding, increases self-discipline, and strengthens self-determination. It illumines, transforms, enriches.

It might be argued that in strict theological terms contemplation is not prayer, and that it could better be called communion with the self than communion with God. Be that as it may, the fact remains that many who have given up formal prayer as a regular habit are finding a new dimension in spiritual experience and power in the practice of contemplation.

Contemplation needs to be learned. It demands concentration, imagination, perseverance. It is a form of active prayer; it is by its fruits that its value is known.

Inward religion is often outwardly expressed in symbol and sacrament. And conversely, inward religion is frequently enhanced and deepened under the influence of symbol and sacrament.

A symbol, simply defined, is an object of sight or sound presented to the senses or to the imagination, and representing something else. A nation flag is a visual symbol; a national anthem is an auditory symbol; such words as "father", "king", "cat" are visual symbols if written or printed, and auditory symbols if spoken. Each symbol conveys ideas to the reader or hearer far beyond the materials used. Mathematics also expresses its data in signs and symbols.

Religious symbols have a psychological significance all their own. Religious truths, being abstract, need to be expressed symbolically if they are to be understood at all. Theological statements, creeds, ritual actions, liturgical sequences, sacraments, are all symbols in one way or another.

It is as symbols that sacraments have their chief psychological value. Such a statement might be considered theologically inadequate. Theologically, sacraments are defined as follows in the Anglican Articles of Religion:

> Sacraments ordained of Christ be not only badges or tokens of Christian men's profession, but rather they be certain sure witnesses, and effectual signs of grace, and God's good will towards us, by the which he doth work invisibly in us, and doth not only quicken, but also strengthen and confirm our Faith in him.[16]

But it is the quickening, strengthening, and confirming of faith *as in inward experience* that is of direct concern.

This demands both psychological and theological comment. Sacraments are not merely symbols. They are something more, and it is this something more that gives them their deepest psychological value. They are symbolic acts which, to be effectual, demand an active response from within and an actualization in the experience of the participant of the truths symbolized.

This is the way to interpret the protests of the Old Testament Prophets against popular notions concerning rites and sacrifices current in their day. The words of Micah are relevant:

> With what shall I come before the Lord, and bow myself before God on high? Shall I come before him with burnt offerings, with calves a year old? Will the Lord be pleased with thousands of rams, with ten thousands of rivers of oil? Shall I give my first-born for my transgression, the fruit of my body for the sin of my soul? He has showed you, O man, what is good; and what does the Lord require of you but to do justice, and to love kindness, and to walk humbly with your God?[17]

Care needs to be exercised lest the Prophets be misunderstood. They did not say that sacrifices in themselves were useless or unefficacious or unacceptable to God. What they did say was that sacrifices were efficacious and acceptable only in so far as they symbolized and were accompanied by true penitence on the part of the worshipper. On this understanding of the matter it can be seen how symbols and sacraments are the external ritual expression of deep inner motives, and also how ritual acts can be outward aids to inward experience.

One of the great passages of the New Testament dealing with the spiritual life perhaps best illustrates this theme, namely Romans 6. The call of the passage is summarized by the injunction in verse 13: "Yield yourselves to God." The teaching of the whole passage can be reduced to five simple statements which need little elaboration.

1. The Christian life is essentially a surrendered life. It is a life dedicated at the highest level of aspiration:

> Do you not know that all of us who have been baptized into Christ Jesus were baptized into his death? . . . Do not yield your members to sin as instruments of wickedness, but yield yourselves to God as men who have been brought from death to life, and your members to God as instruments of righteousness. . . . Do you not know that if you yield yourselves to any one as obedient slaves, you are slaves of the one you obey, either of sin, which leads to death, or of obedience, which leads to righteousness?

In the realm of everyday existence there is no such thing as absolute freedom. Everyone is to some extent surrendered to something, for good or ill. Christian surrender is positive; it is the difference between indecision and decision; it is the difference between bondage and freedom, for such service as it entails is perfect freedom. At least, that is what it should be. George Matheson went to the heart of the matter when he wrote:

> Make me a captive, Lord,
> And then I shall be free;
> Force me to render up my sword,
> And I shall conqueror be.

And again:

> My will is not my own
> Till Thou hast made it Thine;
> If it would reach a monarch's throne
> It must its crown resign;

> It only stands unbent,
> Amid the clashing strife,
> When on Thy bosom it has leant
> And found in Thee its life.

It is true. We are free only in so far as our life is surrendered or dedicated or given to some positive ideal. We stoop to conquer; we die to live.

A warning is necessary, however, for it is possible to surrender and conform from motives of fear or compulsion. In that case it can be a restricting experience. But there is no reason why a healthy-minded person should not make a voluntary surrender to an ideal which inspires him and stimulates him to a life of usefulness. Self-denial is not in itself pathological. Indeed, it is the mature person who can afford to deny himself. Refusal to dedicate oneself may be a sign of maladjustment rather than of maturity.

That fine essayist, F. W. Boreham, was playing a game of dominoes. trying to match the challenge of his opponent's pieces and to get rid of his own dominoes to win the game. And he writes: "It occurred to me whilst we were playing that life itself is but a game of dominoes. Its highest art lies in matching your companion's pieces. . . . It means, of course, that if you answer the challenge every time, your pieces will soon be gone. But, as against that, it is worth remembering that victory lies not in accumulation, but in exhaustion. The player who is left with empty hands wins everything."[18]

Now there are two words in the above quotations which perhaps need to be clarified. They are the words "force" ("Force me to render up my sword" in Matheson's hymn), and "exhaustion" in Boreham's analogy. These could possibly carry meanings which would rightly be labelled pathological; but they are not meant in this way in their contexts. Matheson's was a willing surrender, and Boreham's a voluntary exhaustion. And this is what is meant here in this exposition of Romans 6, when I say that the Christian life is a surrendered life. It is a positive surrender, a willing self-giving.

Religion can create problems for people; but in its best expression it can solve problems. It can lead from vacillation to stability, from restlessness to poise, from the diffusion of life's energies to their dedication by sublimation to high and emancipating ideals. This is what religion is meant to do.

2. A surrendered life is a renewed, a self-possessed (in Christian language, a Spirit-filled) life. It is the difference between death and life, between disintegration and fulfilment.

> We were buried therefore with him by baptism into death, so that as Christ was raised from the dead by the glory of the Father, we too might walk in newness of life.

Dr Arthur Guirdham[19] has depicted man as engaged in the task of resolving a two-way conflict which rages within him. The higher impulses can be served only by the defeat, or, as he says, by the death of the lower impulses. Each person must choose between the life which comes from the death of the lower impulses and the death which results from allowing those impulses to live. This is a psychiatrist's way of saying what St Paul is saying in this passage from Romans 6.

3. A renewed or self-possessed or Spirit-filled life is a unified life, an integrated life. It is the difference between inner discord and harmony within.

> Do you not know that if you yield yourselves to any one as obedient slaves, you are slaves of the one whom you obey, either of sin, which leads to death, or of obedience, which leads to righteousness? But thanks be to God, that you who were once slaves of sin have become obedient from the heart to the standard of teaching to which you were committed, and, having been set free from sin, have become slaves of righteousness.

All too often men's lives are at sixes and sevens. They are victims of conflicting desires and loyalties. As Dean Farrar used to say, they fall between the desire to do right and the temptation to do wrong. But when the life is surrendered to a high ideal it becomes unified within. Thought, desire, and will are dedicated and channelled—sublimated is the psychological term—to higher ends. As our Lord said, when a man loses himself in this way he finds himself anew.

4. A unified and integrated life is a powerful life. It is the difference between defeat and victory.

> For if we have been united with him in a death like his, we shall certainly be united with him in a resurrection like his. We know that our old self was crucified with him so that the sinful body might be destroyed, and we might no longer be enslaved to sin. For he who has died is freed from sin. . . . So you also must consider yourselves dead to sin and alive to God in Christ Jesus. . . . For sin will have no dominion over you, since you are not under law but under grace. . . . I am speaking in human terms, because of your natural limitations. For just as you once yielded your members to impurity and to greater and greater iniquity, so now yield your members to righteousness for sanctification.

To quote George Matheson again:

> My heart is weak and poor
> Until it master find;
> It has no spring of action sure—
> It varies with the wind.
> It cannot freely move,
> Till Thou hast wrought its chain;
> Enslave it with Thy matchless love,
> And deathless it shall reign.

5. A powerful life is a useful life. It is the difference between drift and purpose.

> When you were slaves of sin, you were free in regard to righteousness. But then what return did you get from the things of which you are now ashamed? The end of those things is death. But now that you have been set free from sin and have become slaves of God, the return you get is

sanctification and its end, eternal life. For the wages of sin is death, but the free gift of God is eternal life in Jesus Christ our Lord.

The wheel has gone full circle. The end product of life depends upon that to which the initial surrender is made.

> Measure thy life by loss instead of gain;
> Not by the wine drunk, but the wine poured forth;
> For love's strength standeth in love's sacrifice;
> And whoso suffers most hath most to give.
>
> (Harriet Eleanor Hamilton King)

> O Cross that liftest up my head,
> I dare not ask to fly from thee;
> I lay in dust life's glory dead,
> And from the ground there blossoms red
> Life that shall endless be.
>
> (George Matheson)

Some may say: "All this is true so far as it goes; but this experience of inner harmony and its noble expression in the dedication of one's life to a noble purpose can be achieved without necessarily giving credence to theological formularies and without affiliation to any religious body." Of course it can; there is no denying the fact. But I would be prepared to say that anyone who is dedicated to a high and noble purpose, even if he does not express his dedication in familiar religious terms, is to that extent religious. The reader is free to make his own judgement upon this. Perhaps it is a matter of definition; but to me religion is so human and so natural and so far-reaching that it cannot be tied to or limited by any particular theological formulation or manner of expression.

In my study I have a print of A. E. Borthwick's picture, *The Presence*. It depicts an ornate service in progress in the Sanctuary of a cathedral. In the foreground, almost hidden in the darkness, a lone worshipper kneels over-shadowed by the Presence of Our Lord. I have heard several different interpretations of this, but for me it means this: The Presence can be experienced in the ritual of a beautiful service, but the Presence is not necessarily there. It is possible to have the ritual without the Presence. But wherever there is a person in earnest, seeking humbly, perhaps dissatisfied with past achievement and penitent because of known failures, yet determined to follow after that which is seen to be man's true end—*there* is the Presence. Individuals differ in their understanding of the Presence and may call it by different names. But the essence of religion is not the form of the outward symbol, or the name by which it is called, but the inward illumination of spirit, the emancipation of the life from within, and its outward expression in service.

Modern man needs to learn to worship. If he looks for it he can find the spiritual in and through the material. The scientific method of discovery through observation, experiment, and induction can be carried into the spiritual realm. There are aesthetic, moral, and religious values which material science, however valuable in itself, is unable to encompass, and it is with such values that worship is concerned. In the present discussion it is the psychology of worship that is in focus, not the theology involved in the concepts under review. Theologies of worship are manifold, but what is being attempted here is an understanding of worship as an expression of the acknowledgement of the worthship of "the things that are eternal".

Changing attitudes to worship are interesting. Many Christian people who find it difficult to worship are giving up the habit. Others are finding new meaning in old forms, and these are worth noting.

It has often been said that the ingredients of worship are praise and adoration, awe, confession, gratitude, and thanksgiving. But when God is not thought of as a Person it is difficult to offer praise, to adore, to feel a sense of awe, to make confession, or to render gratitude and thanksgiving. Yet these are such fundamentally human attitudes that they ought to find some means of expression in the religious life.

Some have found a solution to the problem. They do not

cease to worship, but they express their sense of worthship in new forms. Their praise is not the adoration of a Person but the conscious expression of the conviction of the supreme value of Goodness, Beauty, and Truth symbolized by the name of God and manifested in the life of Jesus. Awe becomes wonder—and there is still room for wonder in this marvellous universe which man is only just beginning to conquer. Confession becomes the frank admission to oneself of failure towards one's own chosen obligation to Goodness, Beauty, and Truth, and the admission of errors of omission and commission. Thanksgiving is directed towards others from whose life and work one benefits and upon whom one depends. I know a man whose Grace at meals is a thankful recollection of the toil of those who have made it possible for him to sit down to eat. Gratitude thus takes on a wider meaning.

Worship aids religious faith and stimulates devotion by its rites and ceremonies, and by its use of material objects. Hallowed buildings, ritual acts, liturgical sequences, verbalizations as in prayers, psalms, and hymns, are all aids in providing the "atmosphere" in which faith can grow and devotion can be expressed.

J. B. Pratt[20] illustrated three attitudes towards outward objects used in worship, from his contacts with Hindu people. With little alteration they can be seen reflected in Christian devotion. An uneducated Hindu declared that his idols are not images but Gods. Another, somewhat more educated, said that the idol is the image or picture of the God (Shiva) who is in heaven. A highly intelligent and learned Hindu declared: "The idol is useful in aiding visualization and concentration. It is a sensuous symbol, just as the word G–O–D is. Both are symbols, one tangible and visible, the other audible; and both are helpful to our finite minds in standing for the Infinite."

In the expression of Christian Faith differences in outward forms and symbols are sometimes indicative of different devotional or doctrinal emphases. The crucifix, the open Bible, religious pictures, ikons, flags, and banners are rallying symbols for different types of Christian emphasizing different religious ideas. Think of the different theological concepts expressed in ecclesiastical architecture. The long nave and high vaulted roof of an ancient church, with its distant altar, is suggestive of transcendence. The liturgical drama taking place in the distant sanctuary, the lights, and the priestly vestments of the celebrant who stands facing east add to this impression of distance, of transcendence, of "otherness". On the other hand, the church of modern architecture, designed with its altar (now called a table) in a central place, with worshippers kneeling or sitting all round, is suggestive of the immanence of God, of God "in the midst" of his people. Such an architectural design suggests also the corporateness of the act of worship, the fellowship aspect of the Christian gathering. The very words we use—public worship, service, meeting—are significant in that they emphasize different aspects and different reasons for gathering.

Material objects used in worship, symbols, and ritual have their limitations, of course. There is always the danger of formalism, of stereotyping the ritual so that it becomes the only way to perform the rite; and if the meaning of the ritual is not understood by the worshipper its significance is lost.

Another point of importance is this. It is not necessary to have outward forms or to use material objects in order to penetrate to the Realities which these things symbolize to some persons. To sit in a Quaker meeting in complete silence without any outward aid but the simple quiet room is an experience from which many more Christians could benefit. The Salvation Army does not celebrate sacraments, but I find myself moved by their sacramental view of all life expressed in words given to me by a Salvation Army officer:

> My life must be Christ's broken bread,
> My love his outpoured wine,
> A cup o'erfilled, a table spread
> Beneath his Name and Sign,
> That other souls refreshed and fed,
> May share his life through mine.

Archbishop William Temple wrote:

> Worship is the submission of all our nature to God. It is the quickening of conscience by his holiness; the nourishment of mind with his truth; the purifying of imagination by his beauty; the opening of the heart to his love; the surrender of will to his purpose.[21]

On the words of Jesus that man's worship of God must be "in spirit and in truth", Temple commented that "in spirit" means "(a) with that highest element in our nature which is the meeting-point of the divine and the human, and should be the controlling factor in the whole economy of our being; (b) in contrast with any literalistic legalism, it means a worship of heart and will, not tied to strict obedience to a code, but expressing a self-dedication more pervasive than the requirement of any code." He said that "in truth" means "(a) in sincerity—without hypocrisy or self-deception, but also (b) according to the real nature of God, so as to be free from all worship of God under a false image, which is idolatry."

Ritual, from the psychological point of view, is an externalization and dramatization of dynamic religious ideas. It is also the means whereby belief in a fact or an idea or a dogma is perpetuated; the myth is dramatized and vitalized by the ritual. Thus, the Holy Communion symbolizes transformation. Too much attention has been given to the externals and not enough to the internals of the Sacrament. There have been many discussions concerning the transformation of the elements, and arguments about transubstantiation, consubstantiation, virtualism, receptionism, and memorialism; but in all the arguments the essential part of the Sacrament is invariably bypassed, namely, *the transformation of the worshipper*, the recipient. This is the meaning of the Holy Communion, nothing less, and it is all too easy to lose sight of it.

A sacrament must be more than a symbol if it is to fulfil its purpose; and this it does if it calls forth an active response and participation on the part of the worshipper.

Archbishop Joost de Blank gave a vivid illustration of this when he wrote:

> Most of us will have been privileged to witness the transformation of a spectator into an actor. For years, it may be, he has been sitting in his pew as if it were a stall in the theatre. He sits alone, isolated from those in neighbouring seats, and he watches the well-known performance on the stage (or in the chancel) occasionally with interest, more often with boredom. Then one day something happens. His isolation is broken down. The drama on the stage has reached out to embrace him in the action, as it has from time to time embraced others seated in stalls and circle and gallery. He finds himself involved as an actor, and in his participation he learns to accept his neighbours. He is now as interested in those on either side of him as in what goes on in front. He is now identified with the worshipping family of God. He is at one both with God and with his fellows. He has been converted.[22]

What has happened is this: the drama has come alive for him, or, rather, he has come alive to it. The drama is no longer merely a symbol; it has become a living experience for him, and transformation has begun.

As long as sacraments can mean that for individuals there is a very real place for them in the life of the Christian community. The minister, standing with others in a common priesthood, has a vital and sacred function. In this he need not be ashamed to be called a priest.

8

Caring and Sharing
The Minister as Pastor

Of all the familiar models of the ministry, that of pastor is perhaps the most felicitous. There are indeed some today who think it inappropriate if not obsolete, and that for two reasons: (a) It has no real significance for many, for there are so few pastoral communities left in the modern western world; and (b) where the term is understood it could have meanings that are inappropriate for the modern ministry. For example, it might suggest a relationship between pastor and people that is too paternal, the minister regarding himself as the one caring person over against his "flock" who need his constant care.

The term pastor need not carry such implications, however. In the great pastoral passages of both Old and New Testaments the marks of the true pastor are tenderness, dedication, leadership, responsibility; and these surely are demanded of the minister whose work is that of caring, as "the cure of souls" was originally intended to mean.

Jesus sent out his disciples to preach, to cast out devils and to heal, adding, "Freely you have received, freely give." In modern parlance this threefold ministry may be interpreted to mean preaching, counselling, and healing. And the word about giving freely can be interpreted to mean to *share*. The modern minister cares through sharing. To care is to share.

As I planned this book I intended to include a separate chapter on preaching; but on reflection it seemed better to include preaching in the general work of pastoral care, for in all three activities—preaching, counselling, and healing —the pastor shares his knowledge of the Faith, his understanding of life, and his own spiritual resources.

There are two ways of understanding preaching. Either it can be taken to mean proclamation, the pulpit being the platform from which the minister delivers his sermon or proclaims the Word; or it can be interpreted as sharing. In past generations proclamation was considered the norm, and in some places it still is the norm; and perhaps the element of proclamation will always be suitable in certain circumstances; but to view preaching as sharing seems more in keeping with current trends.

Preaching is not propaganda but a means of communication. For this reason it is necessary for the preacher to address himself to his hearers' needs. But he will not know their needs unless he is in personal touch with them. Gone are the days when a minister could afford to prepare his sermon at his desk, take it into the pulpit, and then return to his desk to prepare his next oration. Sermons do not "come" that way; they arise more effectively from human situations in which preacher and hearer know each other to be involved.

To speak of communication (Latin *communis*—common) is to assume that there is an area of commonness in the experience of both speaker and hearer. The greater the area of commonness between them the easier the communication will be. If two people whose native languages differ from one another have a third language in common it is obvious that communication will be facilitated if both have a high degree of fluency in the third language. If either or both have but a smattering of the third language, then communication will be difficult between them, for the area of commonness is small. Likewise, if one well versed in a subject wishes to communicate the principles of his subject to one who is altogether a beginner, then the teacher will have to find some common ground between them on which to build. It is a maxim of education that one builds on knowledge or experience already attained. So in preaching. But, given the commonness that stems from personal relationships between pastor and people, certain "rules" apply to preaching in the congregation.

Preaching must be personal. The "I–thou" relationship

is essential. There is a temptation for a preacher to regard his congregation as a group or a crowd according to its numerical size. But this would be a psychological blunder. A group or a crowd is a gathering of individuals, and the preacher must remember that he is speaking to individuals.

Preaching must be in understandable terms. The Word has to become incarnate. Concepts often need to be expressed in perceptual language, by symbol or analogy. The hypothetical case, the story, the word picture, the simple illustration, are means whereby ideas can be concretized and given meaning. Such was our Lord's method in his teaching parables.

Preaching must be authoritative, but tempered with humility. If it is to interest and inspire, there must be the note of authority in it; not dogmatic authority, for that could call out an adverse response, but the authority of confidence and personal integrity. The preacher must be humble and human. If his hearers feel that he understands their problems, they will be inclined to listen to what he has to say, but if he is aloof or condescending, they cannot be blamed if they tend to discredit what he says.

A preacher has the right to speak with all the conviction that he can command; but, on the other hand, he has a responsibility to his hearers to leave them free to accept, to reject, or to modify for their own needs the message he proclaims. He has no right to preach so as to imply that his hearers are under obligation to accept his word at its face value.

It is sometimes said that we cannot reach with preaching people who are not in church. True; but it is the minister's duty to make his preaching as good and as effective as it possibly can be for those who do attend. Commenting on the Sermon on the Mount which Christ addressed to his disciples, one writer remarked that he "spoke into the ear of the Church and was overheard by the world". The modern preacher could follow no better example. If he will take the trouble to teach his people he will find that they become able witnesses who know what and why they believe.

There is a popular distinction in some Christian circles

between "the teacher" and "the evangelist". It is an unfortunate and unnecessary distinction. The modern preacher, whoever he is, must be a teacher. We hear too much about "the simple Gospel". There is no such thing. The Gospel is not simple; it is profound. To preach it effectively calls for all the talents that a man can consecrate to its service.

The distinction between teacher and evangelist is sometimes a cloak for laziness; the evangelist persuades himself that he is called to preach the simplicities of the Gospel; he thus saves himself the trouble of much study. If he is an itinerant preacher he is tempted to adopt the method of preparing a few simple addresses that will, he imagines, suit all occasions. The teacher, on the other hand, is tempted to feel that his work is not to call for any response from his hearers; his preaching, therefore, is apt to become impersonal if not irrelevant. These are not imaginary dangers; they are observable tendencies.

It is perhaps less difficult for most preachers to choose topics on which to discourse Sunday by Sunday as they face their congregations than it is to find a message for them. Sometimes a preacher finds himself asking: "What is *the Word* for this occasion? What must be my message? What must I declare?"

Today there is a fresh call to the whole company of preachers, a call which every minister ought seriously to lay to heart. Every preacher ought to ask himself whether his message is really relevant to the needs of those to whom he speaks. He must ask himself whether in fact he is aware of their real needs. Is his preaching governed by a true understanding of their needs or by the standards of mere orthodoxy? Is it really a message? When he preaches, do men hear from his lips the authentic Word or mere religious shibboleths? Time spent in self-examination in this connection would not be wasted.

To the preacher is committed both the word and the work of reconciliation. Never was his task more difficult or more exacting, and never was it more important or more exciting than it is today. For the preacher to speak thoughtfully, plainly, and boldly into the ear of the church is the surest means, ultimately, of his being overheard by the world.

As counsellor the minister will be prepared to listen to people's problems, to attempt to answer their questions, and to help them to resolve their perplexities; he will share their sorrows, bear with their infirmities, sustain them in their disappointments, and help them in their search for understanding.

One of the most serious problems is that many persons have little or no sense of meaning in their lives. When the pastor as counsellor is confronted by such a problem he could find much to help in Dr Frankl's *Logotherapy*.[23] Its central theme is *meaning*. Existence may appear to be meaningless to a person, yet there is a meaning even if he does not consciously sense it; the task of the pastor-counsellor is to help the seeker to find that meaning. If a patient tells Dr Frankl that he has contemplated suicide, the doctor will ask: "Why do you not commit suicide?" The answer may be "I am held back because of the children", or "I could not do it for the wife's sake", or "Because I have not yet accomplished what I set out to do." Such answers indicate a purpose to some extent hidden from or unrealized by the patient, and suggest possibilities for his finding some meaning to life. His children, his wife, or his life's aims might be the very key to his discovery of meaning for him. Each person must find meaning, or, if necessary, create meaning for his own existence.

Logotherapy is both a philosophy of life and a method of healing. As such it covers all aspects of life. For example, on the meaning of love: much that is called love is better termed sexual laxity. Dr Frankl defines three possible attitudes towards other persons: (*a*) There is the sexual attitude. The other person happens to be sexually arousing; (*b*) The erotic attitude, which is one step higher than the sexual: it represents a deeper relationship—an entrance into the psychic structure of the other person; (*c*) The third possible attitude is love itself—the penetration of the deep personal structure of the other person, the coming into relationship with another as a spiritual being. It is at this deepest level of relationship that the meaning of love can be realized.

Dr Frankl deals with the problems of work and unemployment. Any kind of work can be creative, according to a person's attitude to it. It is not only certain types of work that can be creative. Vocational workers, such as doctors, nurses, and ministers can have inadequate and therefore unsatisfying attitudes to their work; whilst those in positions that are not readily recognizable as vocations can have adequate and satisfying attitudes to their work.

A jobless man feels useless and experiences a feeling of inner emptiness because he is unemployed. Unemployment thus becomes a culture medium for the spread of neurosis.

On the other hand there can be neurotic attitudes to work as well as healthy, therapeutic attitudes. A person can escape from reality by immersing himself in his work; he can live for his work and dedicate himself to it to such a degree that, being occupied by work, he has no time to face his other responsibilities. The key to the meaning of work lies in the person's making a realistic assessment of it as his unique opportunity to contribute to life.

An important area of human experience to which Dr Frankl addresses himself is that of suffering and pain. The problem of suffering holds an important place in Dr Frankl's thinking. To a significant degree his philosophy develops from the experience of suffering. But he looks once more for meaning. Having suffered himself, and having made something positive of his own sufferings, he is in a position to make a positive contribution to others. Human life and destiny are fulfilled not only through creating and enjoying; often they have to be achieved in and through suffering. To seek for suffering, or to endure suffering which could be avoided, may well be a form of masochism; but to endure and to triumph over unavoidable suffering is heroism, and the human spirit is made for heroic effort. In the concentration camp the prisoner could say, "I am imprisoned, yet I am free." He was free to think and free to adopt an attitude to his suffering, and in this realization he rose above the sordid surroundings which physically confined him.

These are valuable insights for the pastor. Just as maturity means not freedom from tension but rather ability to live with tensions and to use them constructively, so wholeness means not freedom from suffering but ability to use suffering constructively. The evil in suffering is not the suffering itself but the suffering which results from succumbing to the suffering.

In his healing work Dr Frankl faces the problem of death. As in life, so in death he sees a meaning. He argues that if the life of human persons were endless, this would tend to render life meaningless. It is because there is a termination to earthly existence that man comes to realize his responsibility.

When a person says to him, "What is the good of living? What is the use of accomplishing anything? What is the use of working? It all ends in death", he replies that it is because it ends in death that life has its meaning. He uses the illustration of the sculptor. If he had all the time in the world to finish his work he might find little incentive to pursue it. But because he has a time limit he sets to work diligently and brings his task to fruition. So death can invest life with meaning. It can spur a person on to bring his work to fruition here and now. Life can have a meaning right up to the last breath, for there is always the opportunity to adopt a triumphant attitude to it. Both personal and social destiny have to be considered. The person who has faith in his own destiny and in the destiny of the race can face life and live it to the full and lay it down with confidence when the time comes.

I would describe Logotherapy as a living link between professional psychotherapy and pastoral counselling. Based on a scientific foundation of psychiatric theory, it deals with the very problems which face the pastor in his work. How the individual pastor uses its insights will depend upon the pastor himself and the person he is seeking to help. On a number of occasions I have lent Dr Frankl's book, *Man's Search for Meaning*, to be read by the other person as a basis for discussion; and every time I have found that the other person has returned with new understanding of his or her problem, and sometimes has found the solution thereby.

I earnestly commend Dr Frankl's works to all who would seek to help others, whether in pastoral counselling or in spiritual direction, or who are in need of help to understand their own inner conflicts. It must not be thought that logotherapy is a short-cut method of counselling or healing. There is no such short-cut. Counselling is a time-consuming activity. But Dr Frankl points the way by his sympathetic approach and it is for each pastor as counsellor to use his insights as each situation demands.

Dr Frankl's analysis of man as living in three dimensions —the somatic, the mental, and the spiritual—is a valuable contribution to the work of counselling. It is most helpful when both counsellor and counselled in the pastoral situation understand "spiritual" as that which makes them human. More and more it becomes evident to the astute pastor that in dealing with "spiritual" problems he is really dealing with very human problems. It is the human person who is beset by the problems, and it is the human person who needs to be healed.

Logotherapy is one of several forms of existential psychiatry at present being developed. One of its attractive features is that it was nurtured if not born within the experience of human tragedy, and so is able to make a positive contribution to the cause of human triumph. The Christian minister, entrusted with a message of redemption through suffering, should be able to recognize the relevance of Dr Frankl's contribution to the work of pastoral care.

Professor Roberto Assagioli in Psychosynthesis[24] has carried existential psychology to a stage where its descriptions are particularly valuable to the minister in his pastoral work. Dr Assagioli describes the human psyche as involving a Lower Unconscious, a Middle Unconscious, and a Higher Unconscious.

The Lower Unconscious contains those elementary

psychological activities which direct the life of the body—fundamental drives and primitive urges, complexes charged with intense emotion, dreams and imaginations of an inferior kind, uncontrolled parapsychological processes, and various pathological manifestations such as phobias, obsessions, compulsive urges, and paranoid delusions.

The Middle Unconscious, he says, is

> formed of psychological elements similar to those of our waking consciousness and easily accessible to it. In this inner region our various experiences are assimilated, our ordinary mental and imaginative activities are elaborated and developed in a sort of psychological gestation before their birth into the light of consciousness.

The Higher Unconscious or Superconscious he describes as the region from which

> we receive our higher intuitions and inspirations—artistic, philosophical or scientific, ethical "imperatives" and urges to humanitarian and heroic action. It is the source of the higher feelings, such as altruistic love, of genius, and of the states of contemplation, illumination, and ecstasy. In this realm are latent the higher psychical functions and spiritual energies.

The whole purpose of psychosynthesis is toward the achievement of spiritual integration. It is not a religious system but rather a form of existential psychiatry, but its techniques have a bearing upon Christian ways of thinking and Christian experience, and they are worth enumerating. Its technique of *catharsis* has a bearing upon the Christian practice of confession; its *critical analysis of the self* has a bearing upon the Christian duty of self-understanding and self-judgement; its methods of *training the will* have a bearing upon the Christian aim of self-discipline; its emphasis on *spiritual synthesis, meditation*, and the use of *symbols* has a bearing upon Christian worship, prayer, contemplation, sacraments, spirituality; and its emphasis on the importance of *interpersonal relationships* has a bearing upon the subject of Christian fellowship.

Psychosynthesis is no short-cut to wholeness. It is all-embracing. It cannot be learnt by perfunctory study. It demands all that the student can give to it. But any pastor who is willing to give the necessary time to pursue its study and to think through its implications will find his own life enriched and his pastoral potential enhanced.

A word of warning must be added. It would be helpful if all ministers could gain such insights as are available in logotherapy, psychosynthesis, and other forms of existential psychiatry. But, unless they are trained and have gained professional skill and recognition in the field, they must eschew all appearance of regarding themselves as psychotherapists.

There is reason for concern here. An increasing number of ministers with every good intention want to be used in this field but expect to do so with the minimum of knowledge and effort; and it is to be understood when some doctors and psychiatrists regard them as amateurs likely to do more harm than good. There are amongst professional psychiatrists and psychotherapists those who have a deep respect for the work of the pastor and are willing to acknowledge his place in the work of healing; yet some of these same men are critical of a pastoral approach that does not measure up to the standards either of a thorough clinical training or of a living theology.

In his ministry of healing the pastor needs all the human insight and all the theological understanding that he can acquire. Counselling and healing are aspects of one ministry, and who can say when counselling ends and healing begins? The aim of each is the spiritual integration of men. The very words of the Gospel—salvation, redemption, reconciliation, atonement—all have this idea. They can be summed up in the one word "wholeness". The gospel is calculated to make men whole; and wholeness has both a personal and a social meaning. When Jesus said that a man should love his neighbour as himself, he meant just that. This saying of Jesus has too often been expounded in such a way as to mean, "Love your neighbour but do not love yourself." But Jesus did not say that; he did not mean that.

There is a place for sober self-esteem, and the word of the gospel aims to set men free.

Of course, there is in the gospel the call to self-denial, to crucifixion in the strong language of St Paul; but the entire message of the Cross is one of victory—of life through death and victory through suffering.

The Church, however, is called to the ministry of healing, and healing is a vital part of every pastor's work. It might be the healing of the body, or the healing of a broken life, or the healing of broken human relationships. The work of healing on the side of its ministry to the sick should engage the attention of everyone called to the pastoral ministry. It is not every pastor who has the specific "gift of healing", but many more could be used to bring healing to the sick if only they had a better understanding of this aspect of their ministry and were prepared for the spiritual demands it makes on anyone involved in it.

Preaching, counselling, healing are aspects of the caring ministry in which the pastor shares with others his knowledge of the Faith, his understanding of life, and his own spiritual resources. He is in a unique position; he does not need to wear the cloak of some other professional in order to fulfil his task. The Reverend Dr John B. Coburn has called him "the-man-in-the-middle", the man in the midst of other men fulfilling a unique calling amongst them. He is a man whose calling is to see life and to help others to see life in its cosmic setting, to awaken and sustain the life of the spirit, to foster the development of man in the higher reaches of his being. He is a man with a message. And whereas others fulfil distinctive roles in the helping professions—such as teachers, doctors, psychiatrists, social and welfare workers, probation officers, and such like—the minister, too, has his distinctive role; and until better models of the ministry are conceived there could be no higher designation than to call him a *pastor*.

9

Postscript
The Minister as Professional

A central problem for the modern minister, and one that is rightly receiving increasing attention, concerns the nature of his role in society. In what sense, and to what degree, ought he to be regarded as a professional? When this problem is resolved, perhaps some of the other problems outlined in this book will be resolved.

The Reverend Dr James D. Glasse has made a notable contribution to the discussion of this problem in his book, *Profession: Minister*. He defines professionalism in the following terms:

A professional is identified by five characteristics. (1) He is an *educated man*, master of some body of knowledge. This knowledge is not arcane and esoteric, but accessible to students in accredited educational institutions. (2) He is an *expert* man, master of some specific cluster of skills. These skills, while requiring some talent, can be learned and sharpened by practice under supervision. (3) He is an *institutional man*, relating himself to society and rendering his service through a historical social institution of which he is partly servant, partly master. Even when he has a "private practice", he is a member of a professional association which has some control over his activities. (4) He is a *responsible man* who professes to be able to act competently in situations which require his services. He is committed to practise his profession according to high standards of competence and ethics. Finally, (5) he is a *dedicated man*. The professional characteristically "professes" something, some value for society.

His dedication to the values of the profession is the ultimate basis of evaluation for his service.

At these five points the professions find their common identification in the world of work, and at these same five points professions are distinguished from each other. *There is no way to be a professional without practising a particular profession.* A particular profession must clarify the terms and limits of its life, identifying for the member of that profession what the member professes to know, to be able to do, through what institution, under what standards, and to what end.

... The clergyman studies theology (or divinity), practices the profession of the ministry, most commonly in and through the church. He is accountable to ecclesiastical superiors, professional colleagues, and lay associates for high standards of practice, and he labors for "the increase among men of the love of God and neighbor".[25]

The Reverend Daniel Jenkins gives a description of the minister which is well worth quoting in this connection:

The minister in a Reformed Church is a member of that Church who is specially gifted and has been specially called and trained and commissioned to serve Christ in Word and Sacrament in such a way that that particular Church is able to see its task in the setting of the purpose of God for all His people. He is the representative of the Great Church in the particular Church.[26]

These are the marks of the professional minister—he is specially gifted, called, trained, and commissioned to a representative role.

In the past, importance was attached to the derivation of the word "parson" and the fact that it implied a central place in society. As recently as 1954 Dr John V. Butler and Dr W. Norman Pittenger made reference to the etymology of the word "parson" in their book, *What is the Priesthood? A Book on Vocation*:[27]

The priest, after all, must be the servant of all. The very etymology of the word "parson" gives us a clue here. It is from the Middle English "persone": parson, person. The parson is the *person* of the community, one to whom all may turn for guidance, for inspiration, for help. How could it be otherwise? The priest's people are living and working in the community, they help form it, their problems lie within it. It is their frame of reference. It is inevitable that the priest concern himself with the community even as he concerns himself with his own people in the community.

No doubt there is some value for the minister himself in this conception of person–parson, providing he does not take it too far; but it is doubtful whether at the present time or in the immediate future he will be recognized as *the* person in the community. It is his own personal qualities and his own hard work that will give him a recognized place in society, and then he is likely to be regarded as only one of the various persons who serve the community. Butler and Pittenger write further:

His people require assistance from social agencies and social workers. Then he must know those agencies and their workers, if he is to help his people. Some of his parishioners are on the board of the local Red Cross, and many of them have volunteered their services to that organization. He must know the Red Cross and its programme, and how it works in the community. His people are all interested in the Community Chest, either as recipients of Chest generosity or as donors and as those who serve on the various agencies that make up the local Chest. The priest must know all about the Community Chest, how it operates, what its resources are, what are its needs and its objectives. Again he must help train his people for Christian service in the community. This will frequently mean that membership on a welfare board is the most natural way in which some of his communicants may express their Christian faith and practice. How essential it is that they should understand that the work they do in the community is not merely secular work, but is work done for Christ and His Church. How necessary it is that they shall not think of their parish church as a fellowship that comes alive but once a week. How important it is that parochial outreach shall be strong and extensive, not confined and ingrown. The Church, if it is to be a vital community, must be on the cutting edge of social needs and responsibilities. How often the parish will initiate a work that the community desperately needs and which may not be done unless the parish undertakes to sponsor it at least in its initial stages.

The authors then enumerate a number of examples of what has been done in recent years by Christian leadership exercised by minister and people together.

As far as the minister is concerned, such knowledge of and participation in the work of serving agencies within the community will be facilitated in the future by the development of team and group ministries. Whereas a single-handed minister in a large community cannot be expected to be aware of, and especially in touch with, every organization within his parish or district, it might be hoped that individual members of the team or group will be able to make such contacts in the community as are appropriate to their own expertise and form of ministry.

Attention is sometimes drawn to the number of ministers who relinquish their pastoral charge in order to engage in work of another kind, such as teaching or social service. It is sometimes said of such a man that "he has forsaken the ministry for another calling". This may or may not be true. If he has seriously tried but failed to find his true niche in the ministry, and feels drawn to serve his contemporaries in some other field, then he is not to blame. It is better for him to serve his generation in a sphere for which he is suited than to continue in a calling which experience shows is not his true vocation.

On the other hand, there are some who feel that they can exercise their pastoral calling more effectively in some other sphere, hence their entering the teaching or other helping profession. A word of advice may perhaps not be out of place.

Whatever the reason for the change, the man who wishes to enter another profession should take pains to be trained for his new vocation; otherwise he will remain an amateur in it. He should seek to be trained as a teacher, or whatever other profession he enters, *so as to add that profession to his existing profession as minister*. He should adopt the ideals of his new profession and accept its disciplines; he should make contact with one or more of its recognized professional bodies or Societies until he achieves such expertise as to be incorporated into full membership; he should read the Journals of his new profession and keep abreast of changes and developments in the field. Only by doing this will he find himself accepted and at home in his new profession, for it is by such standards that his competence will be judged and his contribution assessed.

The church-based or parish-based minister is himself a specialist. He needs to be skilled in more disciplines than did his predecessors of even a generation or so ago. He needs a working insight into the aims and methods of other professionals. He must be something of a psychologist, with sufficient knowledge at least to know when a person's problem is beyond his own professional skill. He needs sociology to some degree, for he must understand the workings of society, of industry, and of other concentrations of effort in which his contemporaries are involved. He must have an understanding of ethnic cultures other than his own, and a sympathetic insight into the great religions of the world. In former generations the ordinand or minister reading Comparative Religion did so more or less as an academic exercise or for pure enjoyment, unless he was preparing for missionary or other service abroad. Today, men and women of other races and religions and their families are living next door to him. Their children go to school with his children, and they all play together. The minister above all people cannot ignore them; he must adopt a positive and pastoral attitude towards them.

Some ministers will continue to act in specialist posts, as chaplains to the forces, to hospitals, schools, prisons, and industry. And it is to be hoped that before long adequate training will be available for those who are seconded to these specialist spheres.

The modern minister needs help to fulfil his professional role. For this purpose he would do well to keep in touch with the nearest theological college or with his own seminary. He needs to know about new books on the pastoral ministry and to read the journals which are published specially for the parish minister. A theological college staff would no doubt be glad to help any parish minister seeking further aids to his work.

Sometimes a minister feels isolated, and no man can be expected to do his best in such circumstances. In a very real sense the ministry is a lonely calling. The minister is entrusted with confidences which he cannot share, and he must learn to bear burdens alone. In this he is like specialists in the other helping professions. Feelings of being isolated and overburdened at times are professional hazards with which the minister must learn to cope; but they ought to be minimized in the fellowship of a team or group ministry and they can be lessened for the single-handed minister who makes it his concern to have friendly contact with his peers.

At the present time co-operation between ministers and other helping professionals cannot be organized. There is no machinery and no central authority to regularize such co-operation. But, where the minister is on friendly terms with the doctors and members of the other professions in his parish or district, *ad hoc* and unofficial co-operation is sometimes possible. The minister cannot press the matter; as a rule he must wait to be asked to co-operate. It is this waiting to be asked that some find so frustrating. Experience seems to indicate, however, that where a minister is adequately equipped and willing to act as a *helper*, he is likely to be called upon for help in his own professional role as minister from time to time. But, as always, the opportunities come because of what he is in himself rather than because of his professional status. The minister must learn to be a professional—to adopt the standards of the professional, to work like a professional, to achieve the expertise of the professional, to maintain the ethical ideals of his profession, and to accept the demands and restrictions of his professional calling—and then to realize that he is accepted by society not because of his "cloth", but because he is a sincere, humble, human person, understanding and compassionate, and dedicated to their highest welfare.

If a minister despairs of his calling and feels that his efforts are useless, let him go out to his parish or district and immerse himself in the lives of others. He may be surprised to discover what he can do for them, and how many there are who would turn to him if only he were more accessible.

Let him share their joys and sorrows, visit the sick, sustain the dying and comfort the bereaved, counsel the perplexed, play with the children, encourage the young, befriend the friendless, go where the people are. Then let him reflect. Let him recall the things he can do *simply because he is a minister*. His contacts with other persons are closer and more intimate than those which the doctor or the teacher or the welfare officer can normally establish. Perhaps when he is relaxed enough to see his life and work in perspective he will be inspired to give thanks for the privilege of his high calling.

Notes

1. *Pastoral Care and the Training of Ministers: Contributions to a Developing Debate.* The British Council of Churches 1969.
2. *Existential Psychology,* ed. Rollo May. New York: Random House 1961, pp. 41–2.
3. *Reality Therapy,* William Glasser. New York: Harper & Row 1965.
4. *A Dictionary of Psychology,* James Drever. Penguin 1952.
5. ibid.
6. *Meditations and Prayers: Address to Almighty God.* Oxford: John Henry Parker 1856, p. 156.
7. *Toward a Mature Faith,* Erwin R. Goodenough. New Haven: Yale University Press 1955.
8. James 1.22; 2.14–18, R.S.V.
9. Lambeth Conference Report, 1908, Resolution No. 41, p. 56, and pp. 145–55. (S.P.C.K.)
10. Lambeth Conference Report, 1958, Resolution No. 155, p. 157. (S.P.C.K.)
11. *Confessions of an Inquiring Spirit,* S. T. Coleridge. A. & C. Black 1956.
12. 2 Timothy 1.11, R.S.V.
13. Philippians 3.13–14, R.S.V.
14. *Prayer and Its Psychology,* Alexander Hodge. S.P.C.K. 1931.
15. *The Journey Inwards: An Introduction to the Practice of Contemplative Meditation by Normal People,* F. C. Happold. Darton, Longman & Todd 1968.
16. Article XXV.
17. Micah 6.6–8, R.S.V.
18. *The Silver Shadow,* Essay *Dominoes.* The Epworth Press, p. 12.
19. *Man: Divine or Social,* Arthur Guirdham. Vincent Stuart, Ltd. 1960.
20. *The Religious Consciousness,* J. B. Pratt. New York: The Macmillan Company 1923.
21. *Readings in St John's Gospel,* William Temple. Macmillan 1939, pp. 64–8.

22. *This is Conversion*, Joost de Blank. Hodder & Stoughton 1957, pp. 16–17.
23. See *Suggestions for further study*.
24. See *Suggestions for further study*.
25. *Profession: Minister*, James D. Glasse. Nashville and New York: Abingdon Press 1968.
26. *The Protestant Ministry*, Daniel Jenkins. Faber & Faber 1968, p. 17.
27. *What is the Priesthood? A Book on Vocation*, John V. Butler and W. Norman Pittenger. New York: Morehouse-Gorham Co. 1954.

Suggestions for Further Study

A former principal of my own theological college used to say that a clergyman's library should be a selection and not a collection of books. On this principle the following suggestions for further study are compiled. The list is not intended as a bibliography on the subject, but rather as a guide to a few books amongst many that are currently available in this particular field.

All titles in the S.P.C.K. Library of Pastoral Care are to be recommended. As this series has developed and new books added to it, it has covered more and more aspects of the pastoral ministry in its contemporary setting.

The following also are contemporary studies in the work of the Ministry:

Ordained Ministry Today: A Discussion of its Nature and Role. This is the Report of a Working Party of the Ministry Committee of the Advisory Council for the Church's Ministry. Church Information Office 1969.

The Sacred Ministry, ed. G. R. Dunstan. S.P.C.K. 1970.

New Forms of Ministry: Research Pamphlet No. 12, ed. David M. Paton. Edinburgh House Press.

Pastoral Care and the Training of Ministers: Contributions to a Developing Debate. British Council of Churches Report 1969.

Amongst valuable books from the United States, I would particularly mention:

Pastoral Care in Historical Perspective: An Essay with Exhibits, William A. Clebsch and Charles R. Jaekle. Englewood Cliffs, New Jersey: Prentice-Hall Inc. 1964.

The Ministry in Historical Perspective, H. Richard Niebuhr and Daniel D. Williams. New York: Harper & Brothers 1956.

Minister: Man-in-the-Middle, John B. Coburn. New York: The Macmillan Company 1963.

We Have This Ministry, Robert N. Rodenmayer. New York: Harper & Brothers 1959.

What is the Priesthood? A Book on Vocation, John V. Butler and W. Norman Pittenger. New York: Morehouse-Gorham Co. 1954. Quoted in the last chapter of this book.

Profession: Minister, James D. Glasse. Nashville and New York: Abingdon Press 1968. Dr Glasse's work is particularly important at the present juncture, confronting as it does "the identity crisis of the parish clergy".

A valuable book with a new approach is *Ministry and Management,* Dr Peter F. Rudge. Tavistock Publications 1968.

A small book of importance is *Existential Psychology,* edited by Rollo May (New York: Random House 1961). It has excellent articles by various writers on different aspects of the subject.

Professor Viktor E. Frankl's main works on Logotherapy are: *Man's Search for Meaning* (Hodder & Stoughton 1964), and *The Doctor and the Soul: From Psychotherapy to Logotherapy* (Published in Britain by the Souvenir Press, and in New York by Alfred A. Knopf 1965). The Souvenir Press has recently published two other volumes by Dr Frankl, *Psychotherapy and Existentialism* (1970) and *The Will to Meaning* (1971). Other useful books are: *The Search for Meaning,* A. J. Ungersma (Philadelphia: The Westminster Press 1961); *Logotherapy and the Christian Faith,* Donald F. Tweedie (Michigan, Grand Rapids: The Baker Book House 1965); and *Jesus and Logotherapy,* by Robert C. Leslie (New York–Nashville: Abingdon Press 1965).

Reality Therapy, by William Glasser, is published by Harper & Row of New York (1965) and has a Foreword by Dr O. Hobart Mowrer.

Professor Assagioli and the Psychosynthesis Research Foundation centres in various parts of the world are producing some fine monographs, but the main textbook in English is *Psychosynthesis: A Manual of Principles and Techniques,* Roberto Assagioli (New York: Hobbs, Dorman & Co., Inc. 1965).

The Crisis in Psychiatry and Religion, O. Hobart Mowrer, is published in New York by D. Van Nostrand Co., Inc. 1961. Professor Mowrer sees both psychiatry and religion in a state of flux, and believes that there is need to re-introduce (albeit in an informed manner) some of the concepts of religion which have been overlooked or deliberately rejected by psychologists in recent years. This is a book which deserves careful study from both sides of the discussion.

Dr Paul Tournier's works are relevant and valuable. I would particularly recommend *The Whole Person in a Broken World* (Collins 1965).

The Faith of the Counsellors, Paul Halmos (Constable 1965) is timely. The author deals with values and value judgements in counselling.

Professor Erwin R. Goodenough's book, *The Psychology of Religious Experiences* (New York and London: Basic Books 1965) is a contribution to the general subject of religious psychology. His other work is *Toward a Mature Faith*. New Haven: Yale University Press 1955.

Clinical Theology, by Dr Frank Lake (Darton, Longman & Todd 1966) is a massive work outlining fully Dr Lake's own approach to therapy and giving a complete insight into the theory and methods of Clinical Theology.

A book to be recommended for its comprehensiveness and appeal to the whole Church as well as to its ministers is *Community, Church and Healing*, by Dr R. A. Lambourne (Darton, Longman & Todd 1963). Its sub-title gives the key to its message: A study of some of the corporate aspects of the Church's Ministry to the Sick. A very valuable book.

I would mention two of Dr Harry Guntrip's books: *Mental Pain and the Cure of Souls* (Independent Press 1956), and *Healing the Sick Mind* (Allen & Unwin 1964).

Healing for You, by the Swiss pastor and psychiatrist, Dr Bernard Martin (Lutterworth Press 1965) is valuable for its comprehensive approach through psychiatry and pastoral care.

Ministering to Deeply Troubled People, by Ernest E. Bruder (Englewood Cliffs, New Jersey: Prentice-Hall, Inc. 1963) is another such book. Dr Bruder is Director of Protestant Chaplain Activities at the National Center for Mental Health Services, Training and Research, Saint Elizabeths Hospital, Washington, D.C., U.S.A., where for more than a quarter of a century he has been engaged in ministry with the mentally sick and where advanced courses of training are offered to clergy who wish to engage in this ministry.

C. Edward Barker's book, *Psychology's Impact on the Christian Faith* (Allen & Unwin 1964) is a thoughtful work worthy of attention by those who are concerned with the communication of the Gospel in the modern world.

A book I feel I must mention, though unfortunately it is now out of print, is *Pastoral Care in a Changing World*, by Erastus Evans (The Epworth Press 1961).

Dr W. Lawton Tonge, a practising psychiatrist, has given us a fine book, *The Mending of Minds: Psychiatric illness and its treatment: a guide for families and patients* (Henley-on-Thames: Darwen Finlayson 1970), which should prove a valuable source-book for the working pastor.

A paper-back by another working psychiatrist, Dr Ruth Fowke, is *Coping with Crises* (Hodder & Stoughton 1968). Written in non-technical language it offers help in understanding and helping in cases of mental sickness as evidenced in human crises.

A book which needs to be read with special sympathy and understanding is *Tornado*, by Helen Moeller (Arthur James Ltd. 1968). It tells the story of the author's experience of mental breakdown and her cure.

A first-rate book is *An Introduction to Pastoral Counselling for Social Workers, the Clergy and Others*, by Kathleen Heasman (Constable 1969). Anyone beginning to study the subject of counselling could not do better than to start with this. Dr Heasman is a good teacher and trustworthy guide.

The firm of Arthur James Limited of The Drift, Evesham, has published a number of books in the field of the Church's Ministry of Healing. Three recent works are: *Miracles of Healing: Studies of the Healing Miracles in the New Testament*, by Lewis Maclachlan, formerly Chaplain to the Guild of Health (1968), *Healing Adventure*, by Mrs Anne S. White (1969); and *Miracle at Crowhurst*, by George Bennett (1970) telling how the call to the ministry of healing came to the author and its confirmation in the developing work of the Crowhurst Home of Healing.

Another fine book is *Healing Miracles*, by Canon M. A. H. Melinsky (A. R. Mowbray 1968). Its sub-title defines its scope. It is an examination from history and experience of the place of miracle in Christian thought and medical practice.

Amongst good books on preaching, I would recommend the following by Prebendary D. W. Cleverley Ford:

An Expository Preacher's Notebook (Hodder & Stoughton 1960).

A Pastoral Preacher's Notebook (Hodder & Stoughton 1965).

Preaching at the Parish Communion, Series One (Mowbray 1967).

Preaching at the Parish Communion: On the Epistles (Mowbray 1968).

Preaching Today (Epworth and S.P.C.K. 1969).

Also

The Pulpit Rediscovers Theology, by Theodore O. Wedel. Greenwich, Connecticut: The Seabury Press 1956.

There are two books of my own which are geared to the needs of the working pastor: *The Battle for the Soul: Aspects of Religious Conversion* (Hodder & Stoughton 1960 and 1964. Philadelphia, Pa., U.S.A.: Westminster Press 1959), and *Christianity from Within: A Frank Discussion of Religion, Conversion, Evangelism and Revival* (Hodder & Stoughton 1965).

NOTE

As this work goes to press, a third and fully revised edition of Dr Harry Guntrip's book *Psychology for Ministers and Social Workers* has been published by Allen and Unwin. It is an important work and is strongly recommended.

Index

Adolescent and religion 42–5
Adler, Alfred 16–18
adult knowledge *versus* adolescent attitudes 42
Analytical Psychology 16
Anglican Articles of Religion 77
Anselm 56
Assagioli, Roberto 24–6, 95
Atonement, the Doctrine of 60

belief 34, 48, 75
Boreham, F. W. 79
Borthwick, A. E. 82
Buber, Martin 54
Butler, John V. 100

children 30–5
Christian life 78f
Christian revelation 67
Coburn, John B. 98
Coleridge, Samuel Taylor 70
Collective Unconscious 18
communication 89
compensation 9
confession 3
Conscious, The 16
contemplation 76
Cross, The 53, 89

Death of God 58
de Blank, Archbp Joost 87
Depth Psychology 16f
Dictionary of Psychology 47
doctrine, changes in 66
doctrine, statements of 61
dogma 1
Dogmatic Theology, 66
Drever, James, 47

Electric Convulsion Therapy, 19
Eschatology, the Doctrine of 60

Eucharist 3
Evil, the problem of 37
Evolution 1
Existential Psychology 20f, 69

faith 46f, 50, 54f, 61
family planning 63–5
Farrar, Dean 80
Frankl, Viktor E. 22–4, 92–5
Freud, Sigmund 16f
From Deathcamp to Existentialism 22

Glasse, James D. 99
Glasser, William 24
Goodenough, Edwin R. 56
guilt 38
Guirdham, Arthur 80

Happold, F. C. 76
Harrington, G. L. 24
Height Psychology 26
Higher Unconscious 95f
Hodge, Alexander 74f
Holy Communion 86
Honest to God 58
Humanistic Psychology 26

imitation 30
Individual Psychology 16
inference 72
intuition 72

Jenkins, Daniel 100
John of the Cross, St 54
Jung, Carl G. 16–18

King, Harriet Eleanor Hamilton 82
knowledge 54, 72

Lambeth Conference 63f
Last Day 37

Last Things, Doctrine of 60
logotherapy 22f, 92f
Lower Unconscious 95f

Man's Search for Meaning 22
Maslow, Abraham H. 26
Matheson, George 78f
maturity 41f, 54, 74, 94
May, Rollo 21
Middle Unconscious 95f
mysticism 74

Neo-Freudian School 18

Old Testament prophets 77
Original Sin, the Doctrine of 59

pastor 14, 88, 98
pastoral care 7, 88
pastoral counselling 94
Pastoral Theology, 68
Paul, St 80, 98
personality 4
Pittenger, W. Norman 100f
practical psychology 45
Pratt, J. B. 84
Prayer and its Psychology 74
preaching, 14, 88f, 98
prejudice 4
Presence, The 82f
priest 71, 87
problems: children and adolescents
    40–1
Profession: Minister 99
psychoanalysis 14–18
psychological study of religion 66
psychology, in general 6–8f, 11–15
psychosynthesis 24f, 96f
psychotherapy 13, 19, 94

Quaker Meeting 85

radical theology, 58, 75
*Reality Therapy: A New Approach to
    Psychiatry* 24

reason 33, 56
religion 9f, 26, 28, 45, 80
religious experience 9, 66
religious faith 11, 49f
religious knowledge 73
religious symbols 76
Resurrection, the Doctrine of 62f
ritual 86f

sacrament 76f
Salvation Army 85f
science 1
self-awareness 25
sensation 32
Sermon on the Mount 90
Servant Church 7
shock treatment 19
"simple gospel" 91
Socrates 73
somology 12
soulology 13
spiritual experience 72
subconscious 16f
Sullivan, Harry Stack 18
symbol 76
sympathy 30

Temple, Archbp William 86
theology 61f, 66, 68
Tillich, Paul 21
tradition 1
Transpersonal Psychology 26
Trinity, the Doctrine of 59

Unconscious, The 4, 16f

Value Psychology 26

*What is the priesthood? A book on
    Vocation* 100f
wholeness 97
worship 83

young people and religion 42–5